Well Said and Worth Saying:
A Public Speaking Guide for Church Leaders

WELL SAID & WORTH SAYING

A PUBLIC SPEAKING GUIDE FOR CHURCH LEADERS

C. BARRY McCARTY

Foreword by Jerry Vines

BROADMAN PRESS

NASHVILLE, TENNESSEE

©Copyright 1991 • Broadman Press
All rights reserved
4260-33
ISBN: 0-8054-6033-0
Dewey Decimal Classification: 808.5
Subject Heading: PUBLIC SPEAKING
Library of Congress Card Catalog Number: 90-2578
Printed in the United States of America

Unless otherwise stated, all Scripture quotations are from the Holy Bible, *New International Version*, copyright © 1973, 1978, 1984 by International Bible Society.

Scripture quotations marked KJV are from the *King James Version of the Bible*.

Library of Congress Cataloging-in-Publication Data
McCarty, C. Barry, 1953-
    Well said and worth saying : a public speaking guide for church leaders /
C. Barry McCarty.
    p. cm.
    ISBN: 0-8054-6033-0
    1. Public speaking. 2. Public speaking--Religious aspects--Christianity.
3. Preaching. I. Title.
    PN4121.M339 1990
    808.5'1--dc20

                                                                90-2578
                                                                CIP

To Wayne B. Smith,
A faithful preacher of the gospel
and a great American patriot
whose voice has called the lost to salvation,
edified the Lord's church,
and summoned his country to do what is right
in the eyes of the King of Glory.

Contents

Acknowledgements

My life on the platform began at the age of six when my Aunt Laura gave me a recording of a comedy routine by Andy Griffith entitled "What It Was Was Football." Like most six-year-olds, my mind was a blank slate that recorded everything I heard. I memorized the complete routine and began reciting it to family and friends. Bowing to the demands of my growing public, my mother entered me in the Moose Club's Annual Youth Talent Show in East Point, Georgia. The idea of a pint-sized Andy Griffith doing a standup comedy routine proved irresistible and I won first prize.

The next year found me making the rounds as an after-dinner speaker for civic clubs and church socials. This phase of my speaking career culminated in an appearance before the Georgia House of Representatives. To my mother and to Aunt Laura, I owe thanks for the great advantage of beginning to speak in public before I was old enough to know that the idea of speaking in public had ever frightened anybody.

Thanks are also due to George BonDurant, who introduced me to the fields of speech and homiletics at Roanoke Bible College; to Ed Enzor, Rex Kyker, and Ed Brown who directed my M.A. studies at Abilene Christian University; and to Robert Newman, Otis Walter,

Thomas Kane, and Nancy Metzger who made my Ph.D. program in rhetoric and argumentation at the University of Pittsburgh a great adventure in learning.

Thanks to my secretary, Pam Gilley, who served as a sounding board and critical reader of the manuscript for this book; and to Cincinnati Bible College and Seminary librarians Jim Lloyd and Lori Thornton for their assistance in locating research materials.

Most of all, I am thankful to Pat, a faithful wife and companion whose love, understanding, and encouragement stand behind any worthy thing God has enabled me to do.

Foreword

I read this book Thanksgiving night. I know. Not a good night to do anything. After a bountiful Thanksgiving feast and several hours viewing TV football, the mind is not exactly primed for perceptive reading. Dr. Barry McCarty graciously invited me to write the foreword for his book. I was pleased with the invitation. Several factors gave me an above-average interest in this volume. First, Dr. McCarty has become a cherished friend. His Christian demeanor and spiritual perception have have endeared him to me. Just the friendship alone would be enough to motivate me to read his book.

Further, Dr. McCarty's superb service as parliamentarian for our Southern Baptist Convention since 1986 indicated to me that anything he wrote would be eminently worthy of careful reading. Also, his credentials to write a book on public speaking certainly motivated me to begin reading it—even on Thanksgiving night. Dr. McCarty has a Ph.D. in rhetoric and argumentation from the University of Pittsburgh.

There were additional personal factors which stimulated my interest. Having been a preacher of God's Word for over thirty years I spend a great deal of my time standing before public groups to speak. I am always anxious to find resources which will help me do a better job. Having written a book on sermon delivery myself I have become a student of volumes relating to the speaking situation. Such a volume written by Dr. McCarty attracted me.

I read the entire book Thanksgiving night. I didn't intend to. I know. Not a good night to read a book. But this book so interested and enthralled me, I just couldn't put it down. Dr. McCarty's purpose is twofold: to help preachers, teachers, and other church leaders become better public speakers; to help Christian leaders influence people and organizations outside the church with the moral imperatives of the Christian faith. His book so magnificently accomplishes his purpose that I found myself completely captivated by its contents.

Dr. McCarty begins his work with a discussion concerning preparing the speaker and the speech. He is right on target when he says competence creates confidence. From this beginning he shares, step-by-step, how to put a speech together. From the beginning point of choosing a suitable topic to determining what you want to say about that topic on to the specifics of putting the speech together Dr. McCarty guides the reader from speech inception to speech creation. Along the way he gives many helpful insights about taking notes for the speech and where to find suitable material. His section on sources of material for a speech is worth the price of the volume within itself.

Dr. McCarty then shows how the speaker can gather, analyze, and develop the material of the speech. This section will be extremely helpful to the beginning public speaker. His insights on outlining, adding meat to the outline, writing the introduction and conclusion are very practical.

He concludes the opening chapter with the matter of the preparation of the speaker for the speech. This is a wonderful section which should be read and re-read by even the most experienced public speakers. At the conclusion of each chapter a helpful summary of its contents is given.

Chapter 2 gives specifics about the process of preparing a good speech. The chapter heading "Organizing Your Ideas" points the way to his helpful four-part formula for organizing an effective speech. He discusses the importance of gaining the attention of the listeners. The importance of a simple, to-the-point thesis is discussed. Following this, Dr. McCarty gives the reader practical suggestions about how the thesis is to be proved, explained, or applied.

The reader will also be assisted in understanding the guidelines by helpful illustrations provided along the way. This is especially true in the section on developing the speech thesis. At the conclusion of this chapter a special note relative to expository sermons and determining a main thesis is provided. Dr. McCarty even includes a sample expository message. (Preachers, you might want to try it on for size some Sunday morning!)

The chapter on supporting your ideas provides a wealth of resources for supporting materials. He shows the beginning speaker how to go about finding pertinent information for his speech. I especially was helped by his discussion of story-form examples. My experience has been that stories greatly assist the speaker in bringing the speech to life in the minds of the listeners.

He correctly states that an analogy points out similarities between an idea that is already known and one that is not. This book enables one to learn how better to use analogies effectively in a speech.

The chapter also discusses how to use quotations effectively without loading down the listeners with too much information. his advice on quotations is well taken: keep them short; use them sparingly. The closing points of the chapter are to the point and most helpful: get your facts straight. Stick to the point. Be specific. Get as close as you can to your subject. be sure your evidence is strong enough to carry your point. Know your listeners. all these suggestions will serve the speaker well in all his future speaking engagements.

The chapter on style is an illustration within itself of what good style is intended to be. Style is the way a speaker puts his thoughts in words. Perhaps the great value of this chapter is that the reader learns how effective the right choice of words can be by the example of Dr. McCarty himself. The chapter is beautifully composed. Dr. McCarty encourages us to paint a picture for our listeners. So he says: "Jesus talked in filmstrips that He projected onto mental screens. He painted pictures." Not a bad picture, Dr. McCarty! He advises us: Be specific. So, he says, "Describe concrete things in the real world." The chapter is also made very understandable by his examples from the great Presbyterian preacher, Peter Marshall, and the well-known speaker Garrison Keillor. These examples serve as excellent illustrations of the importance of an effective style.

Dr. McCarty's brief discussion of proper grammar provides a helpful refresher course for the public speaker. I would recommend that all who read this book refer to this section frequently. This section is a storehouse of helpful information about how to make one's speaking grammar more effective.

The concluding chapter "Speaking the Speech: Delivery" is perhaps the best. Seldom have I read a chapter with as much down-to-earth, common-sense guidance on good public speaking. The chapter begins by making the point that good speaking delivery is made more effective if the speaker is thoroughly familiar with the speech. Dr. McCarty advises: "Work on memorizing the ideas, not the words of your speech." Dr. McCarty admonishes us to speak with passion. I like his reference to "fire in the bell." For the speaker to speak out of genuine concern and conviction is almost to guarantee a hearing for what he has to say. Eye contact is discussed. This section shows the importance of and the reasons for the speaker having good eye contact with his audience as he delivers his speech.

Several aspects of vocal mechanics are discussed in this chapter. The importance of relaxation, speaking from the abdomen, proper articulation, and good pronunciation are surveyed. His discussion of the importance of speaking with variety and expression is useful. He shares the various means of achieving sparkling speech such as change of pitch, change of volume, and change of rate. The section on the use of pauses will serve the beginning speaker well. There is also a discussion of meaningful gestures and proper attire. Do not minimize nor overlook these aspects of good public speaking. Dr. McCarty closes this volume with the encouragement to make your speech brief. His closing illustrations are classic. I was merely going to read a few pages. I know. Thanksgiving night is not a good night to read a book. Come to think of it—it was an excellent night to read this one. When I concluded I bowed my head and thanked the Lord for giving this helpful, practical volume on public speaking. That's what Thanksgiving is all about. Take your time. Digest its contents. Put the suggestions to use in your next public speech. I will read this magnificent volume again. And again.

Jerry Vines, Pastor
First Baptist Church
Jacksonville, Florida

1

Preparing the Speaker and the Speech

It is 3:30 a.m. From down the hall I hear again the sound that awakened me. My ten-year-old son, Ryan, is lying on the floor, curled like a pretzel, calling for help. He is burning with fever. I hurriedly dress, wrap him in a blanket, and head for the car. In a few minutes we're in the hospital emergency room. Following a quick examination, a young doctor says, "Sir, your child has a ruptured appendix. We must operate at once. Follow me."

The doctor leads me to a sink and instructs me to scrub up with him. A nurse helps me into a mask, gloves, and surgical gown. Through a glass wall I can see an orderly rolling my son into the operating room. I follow the doctor into the operating room and over to the table on which my son has just been put to sleep.

"We're ready to begin," the young doctor says as he places the scalpel in my hand.

"What's this for?" I ask.

"Why, you're going to perform the operation," comes the reply.

I open my eyes and realize I've just had a nightmare. Operate on one of my own children? Slit my son open, cut out one of his organs, and sew him back together? The idea absolutely terrifies me. Why? Because I don't know the first thing about performing an appendectomy. I have no idea of how to go about it. So it scares me to think that my child's life would depend on my having to do something I don't know how to do. If, however, my friend Rob Powell had to perform an appendectomy on one of his children, it wouldn't faze him at all. Why? Because Rob is a doctor. He knows how to take out an appendix. And because he knows how, the thought of doing it doesn't scare him. For most people, the thought of standing before a live audience and giving a speech is as scary as the idea of performing surgery is to me. And, it's scary for the same reason: they don't know what to do. They don't know how to give a speech. That's what we're going to talk about in this book: how to give a speech.

If you're like most people, who are terrified by public speaking, I want you to memorize this line:

Competence creates confidence.

The secret to being a confident public speaker is being competent in public speaking. Once you know what to do and how to do it, you can face any speaking opportunity with the assurance that you have what it takes to make a good speech.

In this chapter you'll learn step-by-step how to put together a speech. In later chapters, we'll devote more time and space to some of the steps. But here is where you start.

Step 1: Choose a Suitable Topic for Your Speech

A cake can only be as good and as fresh as the ingredients you put in it. If you have bad eggs to start with, it doesn't matter how good a chef you are, you're not going to make a good cake. It's the same with a speech. A good speech starts with a suitable topic.

A Suitable Topic Is One You Know Something About

Usually, the reason you're behind the podium to speak on a particular topic is that you already know something about it. Whether you speak on your own or on someone else's initiative, here is one of the few absolutely unbreakable rules of public speaking: you must know what you're talking about. You can follow the rule in one of four ways: (1) You already know something about the topic; (2) You have the time and resources to learn enough to speak about it; (3) You change an assigned topic to something you do know; or (4) You decline to speak. Short of having a professional speech writer on your payroll, these are your only options.

James C. Humes, who served as a speech writer and adviser to three U. S. Presidents, tells of an invitation he had to speak to a state bankers' association. When he arrived at the hotel, the notice posted outside the meeting room said:

Bankers' Association—Washington Room
James C. Humes—
"Fiscal Econometrics in Washington"

After being introduced, Humes told his audience something he learned while a student at Williams College. Along with several football players, he enrolled in "Survey of the New Testament" because the professor, a retired Episcopal priest, always gave the same examination each year: "Trace and delineate the travels of the Apostle Paul." That meant that Humes and his friends could skip classes secure in the knowledge that they could ace the final examination question on the travels of Paul.

When, however, the day of the examination arrived, the professor asked nothing about the travels of Paul. He gave this question instead: "Analyze and criticize the Sermon on the Mount." The class was stunned. No one seemed to know what to do, except one lowbrow football tackle, named Tiny, who began to scribble furiously in his examination booklet. When the grades were posted, Tiny received the highest mark, a B-plus. Humes asked, "Tiny, whatever did you write on that question, 'Analyze and criticize the Sermon on the Mount' "?

Tiny replied, "Well, Humes, I wrote, 'Who am I to criticize the words of the Master? Instead, let me tell you about the travels of the Apostle Paul.' "

Humes then said to the bankers, "Who am I to analyze economics before this group of monetary experts? Instead I would like to talk about my experiences in Washington, which I have entitled, 'Confessions of a White House Ghost.' "[1]

As a seasoned speaker, James Humes knew that it is better to change the topic and do a good job talking on something you know, than to stick with an assigned subject and bomb. If you know what you're talking about, fine. If you don't know, but have the time and resources to learn enough, fine. If not, change the topic or decline.

A Suitable Topic Is One You Care About

Does this subject interest you? Do you care about it? Are you committed to seeing your listeners do what you will ask them to do about it? The more committed you are to a topic, the more likely you will be to secure the commitment of your listeners.

In 1919 Eugene Lang was the nine-year-old son of an immigrant family that scraped for a living. To save the nickel streetcar fare, he walked two miles back and forth to Public School 121 in Harlem. From those humble beginnings, Lang went on to found the Refac Technology Development Corporation and to become a wealthy international industrialist.

In 1981 Lang's old school, P.S. 121, invited him to give the commencement address to the sixth grade class. Lang began his speech by urging the students to work hard and stay in school so that they, too, could achieve success. About midway through the address, Lang realized that his paralyzingly dull speech was meaningless to the poor black and Hispanic children who made up his audience. Suddenly, he broke from his prepared text and told the astonished youngsters something that changed their lives. Lang decided he would do more than merely urge them to finish school and go to college. He promised to put up the money to provide a college education for every student who applied himself and earned high enough grades to be admitted to college. For Lang and his sixth-grade listeners, it was the most exciting speech he could give or they could hear.

In 1985 *Time* magazine told the story of Lang's spontaneous commencement address and reported that not one of the fifty-two students still in the New York area had abandoned school. In 1987 the speech was the subject of a piece on CBS's "Sixty Minutes."

Though not all of us can afford to give away a college

education to our audiences, we can supply another ingredient that made Lang's message come alive: commitment. Lang knew that it meant nothing to tell those kids to stay in school unless he really cared about their staying in school. And for him caring meant doing what he could to help them achieve the goal he urged them to pursue. In the "Sixty Minutes" interview Lang said that the most valuable thing he gave those kids was not tuition but attention. To give a great speech you must care about your topic and care about getting your listeners to embrace it and act upon it.

A Suitable Topic Is One that Speaks to Great Issues

No one should ever rise to speak because he has to *say something*, but because he has *something to say*. A great speech starts with a topic that will make a significant difference in the lives of your listeners. Tell them something they ought to but don't already know, explain something they ought to but don't already understand, convince them of something they ought to but don't already believe, or motivate them to do something they ought to be but aren't already doing. Unless your topic will do at least one of those four things, forget it and find another. Speak because you really have something to say, something that will make a difference. Speak to great issues.

In a remote, insignificant corner of the first-century Roman world, a group of Galilean fishermen shook the world with their words. When arrested for preaching in the temple at Jerusalem, they boldly told the supreme court of the Jewish nation that they spoke and acted in the name of Jesus, and declared that "Salvation is found in no one else, for there is no other name under heaven given to men by which we must be saved"(Acts

4:12). The Sanhedrin was astonished that unschooled and ordinary men could speak with such courage and power that people embraced their message by the thousands. Their secret? They proclaimed the greatest story ever told. They had something worth saying.

In 1517 a Roman Catholic monk, who had wrestled for ten years with the Church's teaching that sacraments and other good works were the way to salvation, came to the conviction that the Bible, not the Roman Church, was the supreme authority and that people are saved by grace through faith in the finished work of Christ on the cross. Martin Luther nailed his ninety-five theses to the church door at Wittenburg and became the spokesman for the Reformation in Germany. When accused of heresy and ordered to recant his position before the Diet of Worms in 1521, Luther closed his defense with these eloquent words:

> Unless I am convicted by Scripture and plain reason—I do not accept the authority of popes and councils, for they have contradicted each other—my conscience is captive to the Word of God. I cannot and I will not recant anything, for to go against conscience is neither right nor safe. Here I stand; I cannot do otherwise, so help me God! Amen.[2]

We remember Luther because he spoke to great issues. He had something worth saying.

In March 1775, as the American colonies stood on the verge of revolution, the Virginia delegates to the Continental Congress gathered in the Old Church in Richmond, Virginia. Generations of Americans since remember the words of the man who rallied the delegates and prepared Virginia for independence. Patrick Henry's "Give me liberty or give me death" speech lives in our national memory because he spoke to the most burning issue of his day. He had something worth saying.

At the dedication of the Gettysburg National Cemetery in 1863, the President of the United States was asked to make "a few appropriate remarks." His address of 268 words took only two minutes to deliver. Yet it remains one of the most poignant tributes to our national values ever penned. Lincoln spoke to great issues. He had something worth saying.

Throughout history, the great speakers have been people who had something to say. They spoke to great issues. Good topics for speeches come in two varieties: timeless and timely. Timeless topics deal with universal questions and issues that are relevant to every generation. Truth, Justice, and the American Way. Faith, Hope, and Charity. Liberty, Mercy, Goodness, Beauty. These timeless ideas concern people of every place and every generation. They are ideas we act on and judge by. Timeless issues can form the foundation for great speeches. The Bible, history, biographies of great men, and great literature abound with timeless topics. A systemic program of Bible reading is not only good for your soul, it will give you something worthwhile to say as a speaker. A good reading list of classic works will also help. Speak on knowing God, the meaning of life, or choosing between right and wrong, and you speak on issues that address us all.

Timely topics are things that are in the news: current events that are having a significant effect on the day-to-day life of your listeners.

Lowering taxes;
Choosing a President;

Protecting your children from drugs;
Responding to changes in Eastern Europe.

Timely topics are the stuff of newspapers and weekly news magazines. I recommend that you subscribe to a good daily newspaper and at least one national news magazine such as *Newsweek, Time,* or *U. S. News and World Report.* My favorite source for current events is *National Review. Christianity Today* is good for keeping up with religious news and issues.

Step 2: Decide Exactly What You Want to Say About Your Topic

As President Calvin Coolidge returned from a church meeting, his wife asked him what the preacher spoke about. Coolidge said, "Sin."

"And what did he say about it?" Mrs. Coolidge continued.

"He was against it," the President replied.

Like the preacher's sermon, your speech must say something about something. To do that the speech must be built upon a single, significant idea, called a "thesis." To qualify as a complete idea, a thesis must have a subject (what you are talking about) and a complement (what you are saying about your subject). It should be expressed as a single sentence that says exactly what you're going to prove, explain, or apply. For example:

- You can have a dynamic prayer life.
- It's time for America's schools to return to teaching traditional American values.
- Drunks who get behind the wheel belong behind bars.
- You can help your child get better grades.

- This country needs an objective, unbiased news media.
- If you fail to plan, you are planning to fail.
- Congress has no business spending our tax dollars to sponsor obscene art exhibits.

Each of these sentences says something about something. It stakes out the speaker's position. The first thesis not only tells you the speaker is going to talk about prayer, it tells you what he is going to say about it: that you can have a dynamic prayer life. The second thesis not only tells you the speaker is going to talk about American schools, it tells you what he is going to say about them: that they should return to teaching traditional American values. That's what a thesis is supposed to do. It tells the listener exactly what the speech is going to say.

You may state your thesis as a question as long as the body of your speech clearly answers the question. For example:

- What must I do to be saved?
- Is abortion ever right?
- How can I get out and stay out of debt?
- Who is responsible for the AIDS epidemic?

Again, these thesis sentences don't just identify a subject, they tell the audience what the speaker intends to say about it. They won't just hear about salvation, they'll know what to do to be saved. They won't just hear about abortion, they'll know if it's ever right. They won't just hear about debt, they'll know how to get and stay out of it. They won't just hear about AIDS, they'll know who's responsible for the AIDS epidemic.

Stating your thesis as a question is often a good way

to approach a controversial issue before an unsympathetic audience. It states the issue under consideration, but allows you to gradually build toward an answer in the body of the speech. For example, when speaking on the subject of abortion I have often used this thesis:

Legalized abortion is a cruel assault upon the youngest, most defenseless member of the human family: the unborn child.

That's a bit strong, however, for an audience that would tend to support legalized abortion. When speaking to such audiences, I have stated the thesis this way:

In seeking a solution for women with "problem pregnancies," did the Supreme Court's 1973 abortion decision create a greater problem than the one it sought to solve?

I make the same points, use the same evidence, and come to the same conclusion in both speeches. The difference is that in one case I approach the speech as a declaration, in the other as an investigation.

Whether you state your thesis as a declarative sentence or as a question, it is worth your while to craft it with great care. Remember, the thesis governs everything else in the speech. It should be clear enough that your audience understands exactly what you want to say. Avoid vague, abstract, or complex terms. Go directly to the central point of your message. Make your thesis concise enough to be remembered and vivid enough to be worth remembering.

Keep in mind that a good speech is like a photograph. It must be in focus. It should center on one subject, not on two or three unrelated ones. And one good closeup is worth a dozen distant shots. A good thesis focuses both you and your audience on a single, closeup look at your topic.

Step 3: Choose Something Specific for Your Listeners to Do

A good speech makes things happen. It moves people to do something. In the next chapter, we'll see that the conclusion of a speech must ask the audience for some specific action that is within their power to give. If you don't have something definite for your listeners to do about your topic, you're wasting your time and theirs giving a speech. Like the thesis, you should be able to state your purpose in a single sentence:

> Have a regular daily time for personal Bible study and prayer.
> Sign a petition asking the legislature to make imprisonment the mandatory sentence for drunk driving.
> Repent and be baptized.
> Say no to drugs.

The thesis and the purpose statement will affect everything else in the speech. Take time to choose and state them carefully.

Step 4: Get the Facts

To believe what you tell them, your listeners need two things: information and images. The information gives them something on which to base a logical decision in favor of your cause. The images you paint in their minds give them the emotional dimension necessary to move them to action.

You should invest most of your speech preparation time in finding evidence (examples, analogies, quotations, statistics, etc.) that proves, explains, or applies your thesis and accomplishes the purpose of your speech.

Look Them Up

Personal experience.—What do you already know about your topic? Most of the time you will be speaking on a given topic because you already know something about it. Take stock of what you do know. Firsthand descriptions of real-life experiences are hard to refute. Your personal involvement in an event or cause can translate into powerful speech illustrations.

One word of caution here: don't overdo the personal illustrations. If they become too numerous or focus too much on your own virtues or accomplishments, the audience will resent your exercising your ego on their time. But when used with moderation, your own experiences can provide a wealth of strong material for speeches.

General encyclopedias.—General encyclopedias are a good first place to look for information because they can give you a quick overview of your subject. Encyclopedia articles are especially useful to public speakers because they provide essential facts in condensed form, which is how you should package the material for your listeners. Most articles also include bibliographic references if you need leads to further information.

Among general encyclopedias, the *Encyclopaedia Britannica* is the scholarly choice. The current edition has three sections: (1) The *Propaedia* is a one-volume outline of knowledge that also contains the author abbreviation guide; (2) The ten-volume *Micropaedia* contains short articles on most subjects with reference to longer articles in the *Macropaedia*; and (3) The larger *Macropaedia* contains more in-depth information on selected topics. You'll get the most use out of the *Britannica* by going to the *Micropaedia* first, then following up on references to the *Macropaedia* if you need more information.

The *Britannica* is a reputable and authoritative work. Its contributors are among the foremost scholars in the world. Each article is initialed by the writer, whose credentials are listed in the *Propaedia*. This feature makes the *Britannica* especially useful for citing expert testimony as evidence.

The *Encyclopedia Americana* is less highbrow than the *Britannica*, but has a more American flavor. It is known for detailed coverage of North American history, geography, and biography. Forty percent of the articles are biographical. It contains the full text of many historical documents, a glossary for scientific and technical terms, and each century has a survey article on the development of that century.

Another readable, popularly written set is *Collier's Encyclopedia*. Bibliographies are collected in the final volume. Forty percent of the articles are on the social sciences and the humanities. It comes with a useful study guide.

Though aimed primarily at young adults (age nine and up), the *World Book Encyclopedia* is a respectable general reference work. The articles are not as in depth as the *Encyclopaedia Britannica's*, but they are well illustrated and provide plenty of study aids and outlines for further reading. Since simplicity of language and illustration is a desirable quality in public speaking, the *World Book* can be a useful source of material for speeches.

Periodical indexes.—To catch the most current information before it has made its way into encyclopedias or books, you must turn to newspapers and periodicals. No self-respecting library would be without the *Reader's Guide to Periodical Literature.* It indexes 180 periodicals of general interest. Articles in weekly news magazines such as *U. S. News and World Report, Time, Newsweek, National Review,* and other popular publications are listed by subject and author in a single alphabetical index. Book reviews are in a separate section. You won't find many references to religious magazines in here, but it does index *Christianity Today.* The *Reader's Guide* is a great tool for speech material.

If your library has it, the *Magazine Index,* 1977- , gives you access to 400 magazines on microfilm. The subject headings are useful and you can look up five years of past issues at a time. Every two months the index pulls out "Hot Topics" into a separate file for convenience. The *Magazine Index* duplicates the *Reader's Guide* and indexes an additional 220 magazines.

For magazine articles on religious topics, the *Christian Periodical Index* is the place to look. Published yearly by the Association of Christian Librarians, it indexes eighty-one journals and periodicals. The sources are a mix of scholarly and popular works and the index has an evangelical flavor in the periodicals it indexes.

New York Times Index.—For speakers, this is one of the best research tools ever invented. The *New York Times Index* is a condensed, classified history of the world as recorded day-by-day in the pages of the *New York Times.* Because it abstracts news articles, the index itself may tell you all the facts you need about an issue or event without going to the article. Like encyclopedia articles, this index is useful to speakers because it provides the essential facts of a story in a condensed package that you can easily convert into speech illustrations. If you need more information than is in the abstract, the index will tell you where to look in the *Times* to find the complete article.

NewsBank.—NewsBank is a microfilm reference service on current events and issues that gives you access to firsthand news reports from over one hundred newspapers across the country. NewsBank groups complete articles on a particular subject together on a single microfiche. Each monthly set of microfiche provides thousands of new articles within a few weeks of publication. A printed index is also updated monthly. NewsBank can quickly give you a comprehensive look at a variety of up-to-date news reports on your topic.

The card catalog.—At some point, you may need more information than encyclopedias or periodicals can provide. The next place to turn is your library's card catalog. Card catalogs index books, and usually some other materials, alphabetically by subject, author, and title. Most libraries use the subject headings from the *Library of Congress Subject Headings.* These large red books are usually near the card catalog. They can give you a leg up on finding the standard subject heading that your particular topic might be listed under.

Vital Speeches.—*Vital Speeches* is a twice-monthly publication of important speeches by recognized leaders of public opinion. It seeks to cover all sides of current issues of national importance. The text of all speeches is printed in full. *Vital Speeches* is a guide to what issues the country's leading public speakers are addressing and what they are saying about them. It is a gold mine of examples and ideas for your own speeches. The *Reader's Guide* indexes *Vital Speeches.*

Specialized encyclopedias and dictionaries.—The reference section of any library will have several specialized encyclopedias and dictionaries. These specialized reference works contain articles on subjects of interest to particular fields of study. For example, the *Encyclopedia of Mental Health* covers such subjects as psychological problems, adolescence, suicide, adoption, and homosexuality. The *AMA Family Medical Guide* can tell you about diseases and health issues. *Groves Dictionary of Music and Musicians* covers the field of music. *Brewer's Dictionary of Phrase and Fable* is a classic guide to word histories that is worth owning.

Every preacher and Bible teacher should own a good one-volume Bible dictionary. It should cover terms and ideas, places, events, names, and important archaeological findings. If you need to describe the city of Jericho, explain who the Hittites were, or check to see whether the son who succeeded Aaron as high priest was Eleazer or Eliezer, look first in the Bible dictionary. For more extensive information, several multi-volume sets are available. For information on people, the *Dictionary of American Biography* contains lengthy, signed articles about those who made significant contributions to American life but who have been dead since 1965. *Who's Who in America,* published every two years, and *Webster's Biographical Dictionary* are also helpful in locating and verifying facts about important people.

There are hundreds of special reference works that can be useful in finding information for your speeches. The reference section of your local library should contain many of the ones we've mentioned along with other useful sources. Ask the librarian to show you what is available.

Almanacs.—Published annually, these handy general reference books compile information from many sources. They contain charts, tables, and other information on everything from daily living (postage, taxes, metrics, calendars, and holidays) to the larger issues of history, science, current events, and world affairs. Almanacs are a good source of quick, accurate information.

Two of the most popular are the *Information Please Almanac, Atlas, and Yearbook*, which has a good current events section and selected short essays on hot topics, and *The World Almanac and Book of Facts*. I have kept these two books close to my writing desk for years. Recently, I added a third, newer, almanac that has quickly become my favorite. *The Universal Almanac*, first published in 1990, is the most readable almanac I've seen. Besides the usual lists and figures, this work explains what the facts mean and why they are important to you. It is full of timely, interesting articles that add a human-interest dimension to the facts and figures.

Interviews.—Don't pass up the chance to talk with an expert if you can find one. Some years ago, while taking a graduate seminar in history, I wrote and presented a paper on the Communist takeover of China following World War II. Most of my information came from an interview with retired Army General Albert Wedemeyer. Wedemeyer served as General MacArthur's Chief of Staff and Commander of the Allied Forces in China during World War II. Though I thought such an important man would never condescend to be interviewed by a graduate student, my professor urged me to try to see him. To my surprise, the General made an appointment with me. A few weeks later I drove to Wedemeyer's farm just outside Washington, D.C. For several hours I talked face-to-face with the most authoritative source of information on my topic in the world.

Seek out experts. They are not all that hard to find. More often than not, they are happy to talk with you about your speech. They may provide you with important information you would not otherwise discover on your own. Moreover, citing a personal conversation with an authority on your topic enhances your credibility as well.

Other records.—Government documents and reports, police records, information files, minutes and newsletters of special interest groups—a good researcher can find choice material in the most unlikely of places. Use your imagination. When you've run through the list of sources I've given you, ask your local librarian where else you might look. I've yet to meet a librarian who didn't just love a good research question.

Write Them Down

Dante said: "He listens well who takes notes." Though some general background reading may prove helpful in thinking about your topic, develop the habit of taking good notes as soon as you begin your research. Don't fool yourself into thinking you will remember all the good material you have read. Heed the Chinese proverb: "The palest ink is better than the best memory." Beware of spending too much time looking for or settling on a topic. Find a good topic early enough that you have plenty of time to research and write your speech. You may occasionally find a topic that doesn't pan out, in which case you should choose another. But resist the temptation to dump a topic until you're sure it's unsuitable. As you look for the facts, ask these six questions:

WHO?
WHAT?
WHERE?
WHEN?
HOW?
WHY?

Look for specific facts and details from which you can build an interesting and persuasive speech. Index cards are useful for taking notes as you read. They are easier to shuffle and handle. Restrict each card to a single idea or piece of evidence. You'll save time if, along with the information you record, you include a note on the source. Record the author, title, publisher, date, and page number of your source. Use the same format on all your note cards: subject at the top, information in the middle, and source at the bottom or on the back. Always label your cards. The label tells you exactly why you wanted that particular bit of information and how you intended to use it.

Paraphrase where possible, but be scrupulously accurate with quotations. Use quotation marks for all quoted material and for quoted material only. Be guilty of recording too much material rather than too little.

Step 5: Gather, Analyze, Divide, and Develop Your Material

Most of the time, this step will overlap the previous one, getting the facts, and the next one, outlining the speech. You should already have a preliminary thesis for the speech. As you look at the facts you've collected, watch for the major ideas to emerge. You should begin

---

Sample Note Card
War on Drugs—Extent of the Nation's Drug Problem

One out of every 100 Americans—2.2 million—is a hard-core cocaine addict, says a survey commissioned by the Senate Judiciary Committee. That figure is twice as many people as earlier estimated by the National Institute on Drug Abuse.

Because of the threat of drug testing in the workplace, drug education programs, and public-service announcements on TV, casual use of cocaine (defined as once a month) dropped from 5.8 million users in 1985 to 2.9 million users in 1988.

However, the 2.2 million hard-core addicts (who snort or inject cocaine at least once a week) show little sign of responding to treatment.

Currently, 1 of every 5 people arrested for any crime is a hard-core cocaine addict.

From an article by Jack Kelly "1 in 100 Addicted to Cocaine," in *USA Today*, May 10, 1990, 1.

---

to see certain themes, issues, or independent strands of thought that run through your material.

As you analyze your material you should ask several

questions: What would it take to get your audience to understand, believe or act on your thesis? What questions must they have answered? What issues must they resolve in their minds before they will assent to what you ask of them? Answer these questions and you have the major points your speech must make.

One method of making a mental inventory and analysis of your material is to create a "cognitive map." Write the thesis of your speech in the middle of a large sheet of paper and circle it. Then extend lines out from the center and set down whatever major points come to mind. Don't be too concerned about the order or the arrangement your ideas. Just get them down on paper. It may be helpful to ask and answer, over and over again, the same six questions we gave you to begin your research:

- What am I talking about? (Define and describe.)
- Who is involved? (Identify the actors.)
- Where is it? (Place the things, people, or events you're going to talk about.)
- When is it? (Next year, this very minute, October of 1066?)
- Why is it? (Name reasons or causes.)
- How do I do it? (Explain the steps.)

If you sense a logical connection between ideas, draw lines between them. The point of this exercise is to identify the major points needed to support the thesis and to discover the natural relationships between those major ideas.

Another method of analyzing your material is to sort your note cards into related piles. If you created good headings for your notes, you should already have some general categories. Keep a miscellaneous pile for notes that don't seem to fit anywhere. You may end up discarding them or using them in an unexpected place as the speech develops.

While researching your topic, you may find the need to alter the thesis and purpose of your speech. Revise them as new facts shape your ideas.

Step 6: Outline the Speech

When God assigned Moses the task of moving three million Israelites, their households, and livestock from Egypt to the promised land, Moses first had to organize them. Each tribe, each division, and each family had a specific place to camp around the tabernacle and a specific position in the marching order as they moved from place to place. The same should be true of your speech. Your ideas need to march in order before your listeners.

As you gather, analyze, and develop ideas and evidence, you should discover a natural pattern into which your material fits. Eventually that pattern becomes your outline.

Your outline must consist of clear, concise points that support your thesis. Each major point should summarize an argument for your thesis or a related group of examples. The purpose of these points is to help the audience understand, believe, or act upon the thesis. Each point should be a complete, declarative sentence. If possible, make the points parallel in grammatical structure.

However you arrange your supporting material, your outline must be clear and it must be logical. The major points must be such that if your audience agrees to the points, they must agree to the thesis.

Step 7: Fill in the Outline with Facts that Explain, Prove, or Apply Your Thesis and Major Points

You have given your speech a skeleton. Now put some meat on it. Having researched your topic, you should have the facts that prove, explain, or show how to apply your thesis. Support each major point with examples, analogies, statistics, quotations, or other evidence that demonstrates that point. Chapter 3 on "Supporting Your Ideas" will help you here.

Step 8: Write the Introduction and Conclusion

In Lewis Carroll's *Alice's Adventures in Wonderland,* there is a courtroom scene in which the White Rabbit is called to the witness stand to testify: "Where shall I begin, please, Your Majesty?" asked the White Rabbit.

"Begin at the beginning," the King said gravely, "and go on till you come to the end: then stop."

Though the thesis and supporting material form the heart of a speech, it has to start and stop somewhere. Keep in mind that the introduction must secure the immediate attention of your audience and focus them on your thesis. The conclusion must summarize your case and call for action.

Writing the introduction and the conclusion is one of the last steps in preparing a speech because until you know the what and the why of the speech (the thesis and supporting material) and what you want your audience to do about it (the purpose), you don't know what you're introducing or concluding.

Chapter 2 will give you some specific ideas on open-

ing and closing your speech.
Step 9: Revise Your Draft

Only God gets things right the first time. Good speeches are not written; they are rewritten. Ernest Hemingway rewrote the ending of *Farewell to Arms* thirty-nine times before he was satisfied. When an interviewer asked him what the problem was, Hemingway replied, "Getting the words right."

I'm not suggesting you churn out thirty-nine rewrites of your speech outline, but it could take you five or six revisions to get a good speech. Once you have completed your first draft, go back to the beginning. Take a critical look at the introduction, the thesis, the major points, the supporting material, and the conclusion. Omit needless words. Fill in the thin spots. Reshuffle points that are not logical. Clarify opaque passages. Get the words right.

The farmer who refuses to prune his vineyard will have no grapes. Fruitful vines do not grow naturally; they must be cultivated. So, great speeches will not spring from your head onto paper with a first draft. Revising is not a luxury; it is a necessity. Prune your work.

Step 10: Prepare Yourself

Fred, Beth, and Don will all give speeches this week. Don has been president of every civic and professional club in town, so the folks at church thought he would do well as an adult Bible study teacher. Since he is a glib talker and a busy professional man, he hasn't given too much time or thought to his lesson. It was warm this week, so Don spent his free afternoons playing golf, about which he knows a great deal more than he does the passage in Ephesians his class is expecting him to expound. Finally, late Saturday night, Don gets around to putting together an outline for the lesson. On Sunday morning he shuffles into class red-eyed, dull-witted, and using the tiny portion of his conscious mind that is operating to cram his just-finished outline into his head. Is this person ready to speak?

Beth finished the final draft of her speech to the PTA over a week ago. However, she left her outline neatly stacked in a desk drawer this past week and retrieved it only five minutes before she left for the meeting. Though her research, analysis, and construction of the speech are flawless, once on stage Beth begins to panic. She has given no thought to what it will be like to stand before a live audience and give that speech. As she steps to the podium her face comes to a full blush. Her knees quiver, her mouth goes dry, and her mind goes blank as she sees for the first time what the PTA looks like from the front and center of the room. Is this person ready to speak?

Like Beth, Fred met a reasonable deadline for finishing his remarks to the City Council's 9:00 a.m. hearing on the sale of mixed drinks. He also went to bed in time to get enough rest. But unlike Beth, Fred studied his outline last night. For twenty minutes this morning he lay in bed thinking about his speech and imagining what it would be like to give it. He arrives at the City Council chamber refreshed, thoroughly familiar with his material, and ready to deliver with confidence the speech he has mentally pictured himself giving. Is this person ready to speak? You bet he is.

Some speeches fail because the speech isn't ready. Many others fail because though the speech is ready, the speaker isn't. A speech cannot speak itself. It must be mediated through the personality of a human being. That being so, a speech can be no better than the human who serves as its medium.

Prepare yourself for your speech. Get plenty of rest. Study your outline. Spend some quiet time mentally picturing the audience, the occasion, and the place where you will speak. Imagine yourself successfully giving the speech.

The Long View

A young man just starting his career made an appointment for an interview with a prestigious company. He asked to get into their training program for young executives. Besieged by applications, the busy personnel manager said, "Impossible now. Come back in ten years." The applicant responded, "Would morning or afternoon be better?"

Though a course in public speaking or a book such as this one can improve your speaking skills, becoming a great speaker is a lifelong endeavor. It requires the same long-term commitment displayed by the young man in the story. The great Roman teacher of rhetoric, Quintilian, began his pupils' training with the selection of a nurse who spoke flawless Latin! Obviously, you haven't had that much of a head start. Still, Quintilian's point is well taken. Becoming a great speaker is a process. As your ability to use language and your general knowledge of the world around you grows through reading, listening, and observing, so will your ability to move people to action with words.

The English philosopher Francis Bacon said: "Reading maketh a full man, conference a ready man, and writing an exact man." Sound advice. Expanding on Bacon's formula, the following suggestions should help guide your development as a speaker.

Good speakers read.—Reading is to the mind what exercise is to the body. Good speakers read news and current events. They know what's going on in the world around them. They are informed.

Good speakers read the classics. S. I. Hayakawa once said: "In a very real sense, people who have read good literature have lived more than people who cannot or will not read. . . . It is not true that we have only one life to live; if we can read, we can live as many more lives and as many kinds of lives as we wish."[3] Good books fill us with great thoughts. Their words enter our minds and become part of us. Good books also expose us to writers who express themselves with precision and grace. If we read thoughtfully, those patterns of language will become part of us as well. The professor who directed my doctoral studies in argumentation, Dr. Robert Newman, was a master of the English language. A group of students once asked him the secret of his success with words. His reply: "Reading Shakespeare and the King James Bible."

Good speakers read books on language. Grammars, handbooks, dictionaries, and thesauri. Many outstanding writers and speakers have offered up their secrets in books on writing. E. B. White's classic *Elements of Style* belongs on every writer's and speaker's shelf. William Zinsser's *On Writing Well* is good. Edwin Newman will delight careful writers and speakers with *Strictly Speaking* and *A Civil Tongue.* Newspaper columnist James J. Kilpatrick's *The Writer's Art* is helpful. My favorite writer on language is Richard Mitchell. A professor of English and editor of *The Underground Grammarian,* Mitchell takes on bureaucrats, educationists, and other perpetrators of jargon, faulty syntax, redundancy, and similar outrages against English. His *Less Than Words Can Say, The Graves of Academe*, and *The Leaning Tower of Babel* are full of pungent wit, celebrated indignation, and eminent good sense.

Samuel Johnson once said: "I never desire to converse with a man who has written more than he has read." That rule applies to public speakers as well as to writers.

Good speakers observe and experience life.—The more vividly you have lived, the more potential you have for being an interesting speaker. Your adventures, travels, discoveries, high causes, victories, and even your defeats will give you something interesting and worthwhile to talk about. The richer your life has been, the more you have done, the more experiences you have stored up in the imagination, the more material you will have to draw from when you stand up to speak.

Good speakers not only experience life, they take pictures of it. Develop the habit of observing what goes on around you. See, hear, taste, touch, smell. Store up images in you mind that you can draw upon as you prepare and deliver speeches.

Good speakers think.—Speakers must make sense. They must bring a logical mind to the act of speaking. They must have imagination enough to translate ideas into vivid images that will move an audience to see as well as hear what they say. Like any other organ in your body, your brain needs exercise. Carve out regular time in your schedule just to sit back and think.

Good speakers listen.—The first person you should listen to is yourself. Record your speeches and listen objectively to your voice. Note your pitch, volume, and rate of speaking. Work on improving those parts of your voice that are deficient or experiment with changes that make your voice more effective. The rules on delivery in the last chapter of this book should help you.

Good speakers also listen to other speakers, both good and bad. When you hear a good speaker, observe what that speaker does that makes him effective. Note how he puts into practice the principles discussed in this book. See if you can discover and state new principles to guide you as a speaker. When you hear a poor speech, identify what principles the speaker violated and how you can avoid those same errors in your own speaking.

Good speakers write.—Since writing is a more exact skill than speaking, it is a good place to hone your use of language. The discipline of making fine distinctions on paper will give your speaking style more precision. Many speakers keep journals to store ideas, observations, and material for future speeches.

Good speakers speak.—Finally, there is no substitute for experience. You learn by doing. Like other performance arts, there are three aspects to speaking: theory, practice, and criticism. Books like this one can help you learn the theory of making speeches. But there comes a time when practice, followed by thoughtful self-evaluation, will do you more good than more theory.

To develop as a speaker, live fully. Fill up your mind with great ideas and images from your own experience and from good books. Refine your language skills through writing. Listen carefully to other speakers, and speak often yourself.

Summary

In Greek mythology, one of Hercules's famous Twelve Labors was to clean out the stables of King Augeas. The stables housed 3,000 oxen and had never been cleaned. Hercules had only one day to complete the task. The myth says he did it by diverting the Alpheus River through the stalls.

Though public speaking may seem like an Augean task, the basic steps outlined in this chapter make the writing of a good speech possible for anyone who is willing to work at it:

Step 1:   Choose a suitable topic for your speech.

Step 2:   Decide exactly what you want to say about your topic.

Step 3:   Choose something specific for your listeners to do.

Step 4:   Get the facts.

Step 5:   Gather, analyze, divide, and develop your material.

Step 6:   Outline the speech.

Step 7:   Fill in the outline with facts that explain, prove, or apply your thesis and major points.

Step 8:   Write the introduction and conclusion.

Step 9:   Revise your draft.

Step 10:   Prepare yourself.

The rest of the book will help you with selecting good supporting material, arranging your ideas, choosing the right words, and, finally, delivering your speech. As you read the succeeding chapters, keep the basic steps in writing a speech in mind. Competence creates confidence.

Making good speeches is hard work, but remember: the more you sweat in advance, the less you'll sweat behind the podium. Be prepared.

Notes

1. James C. Humes, *Standing Ovation* (New York: Harper and Row, 1988), 6-7.

2. Martin Luther, as cited by Roland H. Bainton, *Here I Stand: A Life of Martin Luther* (Nashville: Abingdon, 1978), 144.

3. S. I. Hayakawa, as cited in *The Writer's Quotation Book*, ed. James Charlton (New York: James Charlton, 1985), 12.

2

Organizing Your Ideas

A speech has two parts. You must state your case, and then you must prove it.

—Aristotle

A speech is not a chicken fillet. It needs bones. Without some sort of skeleton, it will just lie on the plate. If you want your material to get up and walk, organize it. Give it some structure.

A good speech outline should start you out in the right direction, keep you underway successfully, and get you where you planned to be. Beyond that, a speech outline must meet two other fundamental tests: It must be *simple*; and it must be *instantly intelligible to your listeners*. In this chapter you'll learn a four-part formula that will help you arrange your speech ideas into a coherent presentation that your listeners can follow and remember when you're done.

Step 1: Capture Your Listeners' Ears in the Introduction

An audience makes up its mind quickly. Good speakers, like good pitchers, throw a strike on the first pitch. Your introduction determines whether the collection of people in front of the podium becomes an audience. You have, at most, thirty seconds to hook them into listening to the rest of the speech. That's as much polite attention as the average person will give a speaker before he drops a mental venetian blind and starts thinking about something he wants to tell the fellow three seats over, his trip to the home office in Atlanta next week, or whether the wife turned the iron off before they left the house. The introduction of your speech must secure two things: your listeners' *attention* to and *involvement* in what you are about to say.

Attention.—The first rule for securing an audience's attention is don't assume you have it. The first sentence of your speech must crash through the audience's initial apathy, boredom, or inattention and *command* their *immediate attention.*

How? Colorful stories make the best introductions. Thumb through a newspaper or magazine. Note how often an article that grabs your attention opens with a story. In a recent issue of *Reader's Digest* an article on judicial corruption in Chicago opened this way:

> Branch 57 Narcotics Court on Chicago's southwest side was jammed every morning with a motley crowd of hucksters, shysters and gangsters spilling out the door. The place even had its own sweet smell of tobacco and hair oil, booze and cheap cologne. Into this place every morning streamed some of the toughest cops, meanest pimps, the most brazen drug dealers, the most pathetic addicts and some of the rawest hustling lawyers. And, on May 4, 1980, an honest assistant state's attorney.
>
> His name was Terry Hake, and he wasn't wearing gold chains, drawing on a cigar or slicking his hair back. But from this day on, Terry Hake . . . would become what he hated most—a crooked lawyer.
>
> He would fix cases, take money, wink at bribes. He would no longer argue a case purely on its merits. The right people could now get him to drop a case. . . .

Terry Hake was on the take. But for a reason: he'd gone undercover, working for the FBI in Operation Greylord, to crack corruption on Chicago's Cook County. It was the beginning of the most far-reaching federal investigation of a court system in U.S. history.[1]

Reader's Digest articles often open with stories. That's one reason it is the most widely read magazine in the world, selling over twenty-eight million copies in fifteen languages each month.

A bold question, a startling statement, a striking analogy, or a dramatized statistic can also make a good opening. I have often opened speeches on the tragedy of abortion with these startling statistics:

Every three weeks, abortions kill more Americans than did the Vietnam War. Every four months we kill as many by abortion as were killed in World War II. In all the wars this country ever fought, from the Revolution in 1775 through Vietnam, counting both sides of the War Between the States, American battle deaths totaled approximately 669,000. Yet, each year one and a half million American babies die by abortion. That's one baby every 21 seconds.

I once introduced a speech to a group at a secular university on the "Historicity of Christ" this way:

Historically it is quite doubtful whether Christ ever existed at all, and if He did we do not know anything about Him. . . . So says Bertrand Russell in his famous essay "Why I Am Not a Christian."

The rest of the speech was a refutation of Russell's statement. It took my largely agnostic audience by surprise and, therefore, secured their attention.

Involvement.—Commanding attention is only one function of an introduction. The other is engaging the listeners' personal involvement in the speech. A good introduction is like a travel brochure: full of colorful photos that say "picture yourself here." Your opening must show the audience they have a stake in what you are about to say. It must reveal that you are about to explain something *they* need to know, prove something *they* need to believe, or show them something *they* need to do. Each member of your audience lives on an island of personal concerns. The introduction must build a bridge from your topic to your listeners' interests.

Observe how President Reagan introduced this speech on "The Problems of Central America" to a joint session of Congress. Knowing that support for the Freedom Fighters in Latin America depended upon getting the congress and the public to realize they had a stake in Central America, the President opened his speech with these remarks:

> Too many have thought of Central America as just a place way down below Mexico that can not possibly constitute a threat to our well-being. And that is why I have asked for this session. Central America's problems do directly affect the security and the well-being of our own people. . . . El Salvador is nearer to Texas than Texas is to Massachusetts. Nicaragua is just as close to Miami, San Antonio, San Diego and Tucson as those cities are to Washington, where we are gathered tonight.[2]

Make it the aim of your introduction to capture your listener's ears and show them they have a stake in what you are about to say. If you don't command their attention then, you may not get another chance.

Step 2: Make One Simple, Bold Point: The Thesis

When Winston Churchill's father died in 1895, Bourke Cockran, an American politician and trial lawyer, became Churchill's surrogate father. An outstanding public speaker, Cockran gave this advice to young Churchill: "Make one simple bold point and keep pounding at it with many illustrations and examples."[3] That's not a bad formula for a great speech.

American theatrical producer David Belasco once said: "If you can't write your idea on the back of my calling card, you don't have a clear idea."

Good speeches make one simple, bold point. That point is called the *thesis*. It is a single declarative sentence or question that states as precisely and as vividly as possible the central theme of your speech. The thesis brings your topic into focus. It tells your listeners exactly *what* you are talking about and *what you are saying about it*. It gives them one clear, concise, unforgettable reason to say "yes" to whatever you ask them to do in the speech. This one simple, bold point is the thumbtack with which you pin your speech to the bulletin board in your listener's mind. Keep it short, simple, and sharp enough to stick. For example:

- Strong families make a strong nation.
- The modern welfare state is organized theft.
- Every Christian should be a soul-winner.
- Burning the American flag ought to be a crime.
- Good leaders learn to delegate.

If you can't state the essential idea of your speech in a single sentence, then you don't know what you want to say. And if you don't know what you want to say, neither will your audience.

The thesis should come early in the speech. The attention span of the modern listener is too short to waste time waiting for the audience to figure out what you're up to. The audience is not interested in watching you buzz the field. They want to know where you're going to land. Don't keep them guessing. As soon as you have secured their attention and involvement in the introduction, tell them why you are behind the podium. State your thesis.

You should then follow the statement of your thesis with a brief preview of the major points you will make in the body of the speech. To preview the major points you simply state, in order, what the major points of your speech will be. This gives your listeners a road map, enabling them to comprehend the speech as a whole and to follow your case more easily. Once the listener knows your thesis and major points, he is ready to hear the speech.

Step 3: Prove, Explain, or Apply the Thesis

After you state the thesis, your listeners are interested in only one thing: "What have you got to go on"? You must make good your claim. The body of a speech should contain the specific facts and details (examples, analogies, quotations, statistics, and other pieces of evidence) that prove, explain, or apply your thesis. You must tell them:

WHO?
WHAT?
WHERE?
WHEN?
HOW?
WHY?

Arrange your supporting material into two to five major points, each of which summarizes an argument or a related group of examples, analogies, statistics, etc. Like the thesis, the major points should be stated as complete sentences. For example, note how the following specific instances support a major point in a speech to challenge young people to leadership:

Major Point: *Many men and women have attained great achievements before they were thirty years of age.*
- At that age Elizabeth Barrett Browning had published two volumes of poems.
- Margaret Mitchell had finished half of *Gone with the Wind.*
- Mozart had published over 200 musical compositions.
- Alexander Graham Bell had invented the telephone.
- Henry Ford had produced his first automobile.
- Computer software genius Bill Gates had founded Microsoft Corporation, which made him America's youngest billionaire.

Each of the specific instances above supports the major point. The major point in turn supports the thesis of the speech, "You can be a leader."

Below is an abbreviated outline of a lecture I have given on the resurrection of Jesus. The body of the speech divides the evidence into five major points. The major points, and the evidence they summarize, support the thesis, which in this case is a question. If the listener accepts the evidence, then he will accept the major points. If he accepts the major points, then he must answer yes to the question posed by the thesis.

Thesis: Was Jesus Resurrected from the Dead?
1. *He was dead.*
- The medical evidence of John 19:31-35.
- The centurion witnessed His death.
- The Roman authorities pronounced Him dead.
- No one questioned the fact then or during the lifetime of the original witnesses.
2. *He was buried in a sealed, guarded tomb.*
- The tomb was "made sure." The Greek term *asphalizo* (used three times in Matt. 27:62-66) is the same term classical

writers used to describe a fortress.

- The tomb was secured by a large stone, a seal, and a Roman guard detail.

3. *On the third day His body was no longer in the tomb.*

- All four Gospels say the tomb was empty.
- The Roman guards say it was empty.
- The Jewish leaders made up stories to explain why it was empty.
- On Pentecost, no one in Jerusalem contradicted the fact when Peter declared that Jesus had risen and that the tomb was empty.

4. *Over 500 witnesses saw Him alive.*

- The New Testament records eleven separate appearances over forty days to more than 500 people.
- The witnesses had hard empirical evidence they had seen Jesus. Luke uses the word "many infallible proofs" (Greek *tekmeria*). Aristotle uses the same word to describe an argument based on irrefutable evidence.
- Jesus ate with several witnesses and gave other physical evidence that He was alive.

5. *His disciples were radically changed.*

- Thomas was changed from a doubter to a believer.
- Peter was changed from a fearful denier to a bold proclaimer.
- James, the Lord's half brother, was changed from a despiser to an apostle.
- Even Saul, an enemy of the church, was changed from a zealous persecutor to an apostle.

To keep your speech outline as simple as possible, make the thesis and the major points the only *general assertions* in the speech. The rest of your material should consist of *specific* examples, facts, and figures that illustrate the thesis and the major points.

One other caution: *stay away from subpoints.* No one is going to follow you down to Roman numeral IV, subpoint C, paragraph 2, item (a)(iii). A thesis and two to five major points are all the general ideas an audience can be expected to juggle during a single speech. Keep your outline simple.

The major points of a speech should always form a consistent pattern of thought. Whenever possible, word your points so that they are parallel. For example, Mike Shannon's sermon on the apostle Paul's priorities, from Philippians 1:12-30, has major points that are both parallel and alliterative:

Thesis: Paul Knew Where to Place His Priorities.
1. His mission mattered more than his problems, verses 12-14.
2. His message mattered more than his pride, verses 15- 18.
3. His Master mattered more than his person, verses 19- 26.[4]

Though most speeches have several major points, don't underestimate the power of a simple one-point outline. In a one-point speech the thesis is the *only* general statement in the speech and the body of the speech consists of specific illustrations that directly support the thesis. It is the simplest, cleanest kind of outline for a speech.

During the 1984 presidential campaign, I heard E. V. Hill, minister of the Mount Zion Missionary Baptist Church in Los Angeles, deliver a stem-winder of a speech to a national political gathering. His address was a simple one-point speech that repeated the thesis after each illustration:

I wish to thank God and you for this honor and privilege. With this privilege I wish to say that I will again support wholeheartedly the reelection of Ronald Reagan as President of these United States. (Applause and cheers.)

Several weeks ago, I made this known to a young colleague of mine in California. He immediately challenged me and asked, "Doctor Hill, do you think we can stand four more years of Ronald Reagan?"

I in turn said to him, "Let's look at the record." Under Ronald Reagan, six and a half million new jobs have been created and over 107 million Americans are working today. I can stand four more years of this. (Applause and cheers.)

The Carter-Mondale recession gave us interest rates as high as twenty-one percent, making it virtually impossible for the poor and the middle-income families to buy a home. Today, still too high, but four years later, the prime interest rate is thirteen. That's down eight points from where it was. Yes, I can stand four more years of this. (Applause and cheers.)

In the late 70s, a word heretofore not generally known came into every household and affected every life-style. It was called *inflation.* It rose under the Democratic Administration to thirteen percent and under this President, it has fallen to four percent in the last two and a half years. I can stand four more years of this. (Applause and cheers.)

In education, for the first time in twenty years, rather than graduating functionally illiterates, the scholastic achievement test scores are now rising and, yes, we need four more years of that. (Applause and cheers.)

This President, this President believes that black colleges must survive and has increased funding to black colleges eleven percent. I can stand four more years of that. (Applause and cheers.)

... Yes, my young friends, I can stand, I need, America needs four more years of Ronald Reagan. (Applause and cheers.)[5]

Whatever pattern you choose, your listeners will appreciate your letting them know when you go from one point to the next. Words such as "first," "second," "and finally" are *signposts* that tell the listener you're moving on to the next point. Signposts should be clear, but not mechanical.

Step 4: Conclude the Speech by Summarizing and Calling for Action

Races are won at the tape. So are speeches. The last minute of your speech will determine much of the effect it will have on the lives and actions of your listeners. You should end on a forceful, confident note. Close the sale by summarizing your case and calling for action.

Summarize.—Leave your listeners with a mental outline of your speech. As you bring the speech to a close, summarize it by restating your thesis and major points. A good summary reminds the audience of what you set out to do and helps them remember the arguments you used to prove your case.

Call for action!—The marksman needs a target. The traveler needs a destination. The speaker, too, must have a goal. You must have something definite for your listeners to *do* about your topic. If you can't tell them what to do about what you've said, you're wasting your time and theirs giving the speech. When you come to the end of the speech, your listeners need more than a simple review of your major points. You must answer the audience's question: "SO WHAT?"

You introduced your subject in a manner that arrested the audience's attention and commanded their serious interest. But that's not enough. You stated your case clearly. But that's not enough. You illustrated your speech with enough concrete cases to carry conviction. But that's not enough. In the conclusion, your audience wants to know: What now? Where do we go from here? What do you want us to do about all this? Ask them for some *specific action* that is within their power to give: Join! Give! Vote! Write! Buy! Boycott! Enlist! Investigate! Acquit! Convict! Repent! Arise and be baptized!

The Bible is filled with speeches and sermons that gave people something specific to do. In the Sermon on the Mount, Jesus told His listeners: "Let your light shine before men. . . . Go and be reconciled to your brother. . . . If someone strikes you on the right cheek, turn to him the other also. . . . If someone forces you to go one mile, go with him two miles. . . . Give to the one who asks you, and do not turn away from the one who wants to borrow from you. . . . Love your enemies and pray for those who persecute you. . . . Ask . . . seek . . . knock. . . ."

Effective speakers give their listeners something to do. They ask for action. One of my favorite evangelistic preachers, O. George Stansberry, concludes his sermons with plain, persuasive invitations to accept Christ. In one sermon, he closes by stepping to one side of the pulpit and saying:

> If Jesus Christ were to appear in bodily form and stand where I have been standing and invite you to come, would you come? If He were to offer His nail-scarred hands [he spreads his hands] and say, "Come unto me, all ye who labor and are heavy laden and I will give you rest," would you come? What will your answer be now?[6]

In another sermon, Stansberry closes with this invitation:

> God has already mentioned the very day that He wants you to become a Christian. That day is [he mentions the present day, month, and year]. Do you know where that is found in the Bible? In Hebrews 3:15, God

says, "While it is said, Today, if ye will hear his voice, harden not your hearts [KJV]." What day is today? [He mentions the date again.] Then this is the actual day that God intends for you to decide for Christ.[7]

Don't come to the end of a sermon or a speech and ramble around rehashing the speech rather than bringing it to a definite end. Park the getaway car on the curb before you start! Know exactly how you're going to get out of your speech. Have a concise, persuasive ending and use it.

Pay Attention to the Three Most Important Sentences in Your Speech

The three most important sentences in any public address are the first sentence, the thesis, and the last sentence. The thesis states your case and governs everything else you say. The first sentence makes the first impression. The last sentence is the thought you leave with your listeners. It will be worth your while to craft these three sentences with care.

A Sample Speech

The following is an example of a two-minute speech following the basic four-part outline described in this chapter:

Introduction
  Last month a man in Chicago was offered a million dollars for an invention he had developed *in his spare time*.
  That story captures our attention because it confronts us with the possibilities of *our* spare time.

Thesis
  Did you ever stop to think that most of the world's

great men have achieved their true life work, not in the course of regular occupations, but—*in their spare time*?

Body

A tired rail splitter crouched over his tattered books by candlelight at the day's end; preparing for his future, instead of snoring or daydreaming like his friends. Lincoln cut out his path to later immortality—*in his spare time.*

An underpaid and overworked telegraph clerk stole hours from sleep or from play, at night, trying to crystallize into reality certain fantastic dreams in which he had faith. Today we light our streets and homes with a device that Edison invented—*in his spare time.*

A restless instructor in an obscure college varied the drudgery he hated by spending his evenings and holidays tinkering with a strange invention of his, at which his fellow teachers laughed. But Alexander Graham Bell invented the telephone—*in his spare time.*

Conclusion

Gentlemen, you, too have spare time. The man who says: "I would do such and such a great thing, if only I had time!" would do nothing if he had all the time on the calendar. There is always time—*spare time*—at the disposal of every human who has the energy to use it. USE IT![8]

A Special Note on Expository Sermons and Bible Lessons

Expository sermons and Bible lessons are an important speaking task for church leaders. The purpose of biblical exposition is to explain, interpret, and apply a passage of Scripture to the day to day lives of your listeners. To organize a Bible lesson or sermon, follow these steps:

1. Discover the overarching idea of the passage. State the central message of the text, your *thesis*.
2. Discover the independent strands of thought within the passage. Reduce these independent strands of thought to their irreducible number. Keep the structure as simple and uncomplicated as possible.
3. Arrange the ideas in order of dominance, importance, or logical progression.
4. Express your thesis and major points as complete sentences that are natural and forceful.
5. Make a relevant application of the message to your listeners.

The following is a short magazine article adapted from an expository sermon. The introduction, illustrations, and conclusion have been condensed, but the thesis and major points remain the same as the full twenty-five minute sermon. The basic structure of this outline should give you some idea of how an expository sermon or Bible lesson should capture the overarching idea and expose the independent strands of thought within a passage. The Scripture text is included so that you can see the relationship of the passage to the outline.

"Called to New Life"

You were taught, with regard to your former way of life, to put off your old self, which is being corrupted by its deceitful desires; to be made new in the attitude of your minds; and to put on the new self, created to be like God in true righteousness and holiness. Therefore each of you must put off falsehood and speak truthfully to his neighbor, for we are all members of one body. In your anger do not sin: Do not let the sun go down while you are still angry, and do not give the devil a foothold. He who has been stealing must steal no longer, but must work, doing something useful with his own hands, that he may have something to share with those in need. Do not let any unwholesome talk come out of your mouths, but only what is helpful for building others up according to their needs, that it may benefit those who listen. And do not grieve the Holy Spirit of God, with whom you were sealed for the day of redemption. Get rid of all bitterness, rage and anger, brawling and slander, along with every form of malice. Be kind and compassionate to one another, forgiving each other, just as in Christ God forgave you (Eph. 4:22-32).

In Ephesians 4 Paul compares the change in life-style that accompanies conversion to a change of clothes. He gives five specific ways we are to *put off the old self and put on the new.*

1. *Tell the truth* (4:25).

The old self lies. The new self tells the truth. The phrase "put off" means to strip away and discard. Like a dirty, ragged garment so soiled and torn that it is beyond cleaning or repair, we are to be rid of lying.

Why? Because we are members of the same body. One of the debilitating effects of some forms of leprosy is a progressive anesthesia of the skin. Lepers randomly burn and cut themselves because the nerves in their extremities no longer tell the brain that they have touched something hot or sharp. Unless the parts of a body tell each other the truth, the body suffers. Likewise, in a family, a church, or a community of people, the body suffers when the parts lie to one another and it benefits when they tell the truth. God calls us to put away lying and tell the truth.

2. *Tame your temper* (4:26-27).

The old self has a bad temper. The new self's anger is always righteous. This nation aborts 1.5 million babies every year. There are more retail outlets for pornography than McDonald's restaurants. On any given weekend, every tenth car you pass on the road has a drunk driver behind the wheel. Those things ought to make you angry. They are things decent people cannot tolerate, and God expects us to have enough righteous indignation to see them changed. But sinful, self-centered wrath that gives the devil room to work has no part in the new life. Put away your temper, but keep your righteous anger that is intolerant of those things God Himself hates.

3. *Be a giver, not a taker* (4:28).

The old self steals. The new self works and gives. For the Christian, honesty is not the best policy. It is the only policy. Obviously, burglary, shoplifting, and holding up convenience stores are not acceptable practices in the Christian life. But neither is cheating the IRS, defaulting on a loan, or knocking off work a little early because the boss isn't looking. When you take or fail to render what belongs to another, you are a thief. Paul says our life should be marked by useful labor, seeking every opportunity to give to rather than to take from others.

4. *Watch your words* (4:29).

The old self has a foul mouth, but the new self blesses those to whom we speak. The new self takes care that no "unwholesome words" come out of our mouths. The term here for "unwholesome" is *sapros*. The Greeks used it to describe rotten trees, rotten fruit, or rotten fish. Would you put a mushy, blackened piece of rotten fruit in your mouth? Would you eat a rotten fish that had been stinking on the beach for three weeks? No, you wouldn't think of putting something rotten *into* your mouth! Then neither should you allow anything rotten to come *out of* your mouth. Vulgar, dishonest, or unkind words have no part in the new life. Ask yourself: Do my words bless or curse those to whom I speak? Does my speech tear down or build up?

5. *Be forgiving and kind* (4:31-32).

The old self is hateful and bitter, but the new self is forgiving and kind. We are to put away bitterness (a sour spirit that finds little good in life), rage (passionate hatred), anger (a settled, sullen hostility toward others), brawling (shouting quarrels), slander (anything said to destroy another's reputation), and malice (the desire to see others suffer).

In contrast, the new self forgives as God has forgiven us. How is that? Psalm 103:12 declares: "As far as the east is from the west, so far [hath] he removed our transgressions from us." In Jeremiah 31:34 God says, "I will remember their sins no more." Micah 7:19 tells us He has cast our sins "into the depths of the sea." No room for grudges, score sheets, or harboring resentment there. If an absolutely righteous God can forgive us that completely, we can forgive one another.

But, we are to do more than merely forgive. We are to be kind and tender-hearted. In December of 1984 my wife and I had twin boys born three months prematurely. Five days later, I sat in the Neonatal Intensive Care unit of Kings Daughters Hospital in Norfolk, Virginia, and rocked my son, Austin, while he died in my arms. It was the saddest moment of my life. As I sat weeping and broken, I sensed someone kneel beside me. It was Karen Katz, the nurse in charge that night. She put her arms around me and said, "I'm so sorry. I have children too." I cannot express how much the kindness of this woman meant to me that night. The world is full of broken, hurting people waiting for our touch. Part of the new life is replacing the old, sinful self with the forgiving, kind-hearted love of God.

Conclusion

In each of these ways God calls us to put off the old man and put on the new. As George MacDonald expressed it:

"The Son of God became a man so that men might become Sons of God."[9]

Summary

Our four steps for speech organization give you a formula for arranging the ideas in your speech into a simple, intelligible pattern. For a successful speech, remember:

Step 1. Capture your listeners' ears in the introduction.

Step 2. Make one simple bold point: the thesis.

Step 3. Prove, explain, or apply the thesis.

Step 4. Conclude the speech by summarizing and calling for action.

Notes

1. Anne Keegan, "Sting in Cook County," *Reader's Digest*, June 1990, 9-10.

2. Ronald Reagan, "The Problems in Central America," *Vital Speeches*, May 15, 1983, 450.

3. James C. Humes, "Speechwriting: An Acquired Art," *Campaigns and Elections*, Winter 1981, 20.

4. J. Michael Shannon and Robert C. Shannon, *Expository Preaching* (Cincinnati: Standard Publishing, 1982), 98.

5. *Proceedings of the Thirty-Third Republican National Convention* (Washington, D.C.: Republican National Committee, 1984), 368-71.

6. O. George Stansberry, "How to Offer the Invitation," *Christian Standard*, June 3, 1990, 10.

7. Ibid., 11.

8. This example is adapted from Richard C. Borden, *Public Speaking—As Listeners Like It!* (New York: Harper and Row, 1935), 14-15.

9. C. Barry McCarty, "Called to New Life," *Christian Standard*, May 14, 1989, 17.

3

Supporting Your Ideas:
How to Prove Your Case

You've just settled down to watch a syndicated rerun of the popular television series "Dragnet." Sergeant Joe Friday and his partner, Officer Gannon, are dispatched to investigate a bank robbery. They arrive at the scene and begin questioning a lady who saw the whole thing from across the street.

"Can you tell us what happened at the bank this morning," Friday asks.

"Why, yes, Officer," she responds, "what do you want to know?"

"Just the facts, Ma'am," Friday says, "just the facts."

Friday then questions the witness about who did what to whom, and where, and when. If she strays from a question or volunteers a hasty conclusion of her own, Friday reminds her to give them "just the facts."

Your listeners are a lot like Joe Friday. Once you make a general assertion or claim in a thesis or major point, they want to know the facts that support your assertion. It is not enough that you simply tell the truth. You must demonstrate that you have done so. Your listeners need evidence to justify the ideas you ask them to believe and the actions you ask them to take.

The following rules will help you select credible, interesting material to persuade your listeners and to keep their attention so that they can be persuaded.

Types of Supporting Material

1. Facts and Figures

Facts are the furniture of the universe. They are things that exist or are known to have happened. They are basic truths about what is there. All types of supporting material use facts and figures. For our purposes here, the difference between *facts and figures* as a category and other types of supporting material is brevity. *Facts and figures* are short, concrete, objective statements about things that exist in the real world. A plain, unadorned factual statement is the simplest, most immediate way to prove a point. Here are some examples:

- The largest living organism is a 274-foot tree in Sequoia National Park, California. The smallest is a Mycoplasma virus that is 0.000004 inch in diameter.
- There are 206 bones in the human body.
- Small businesses employ 55 percent of the private work force and produce 62 percent of new jobs.
- Rudyard Kipling won the 1907 Nobel Prize for Literature.
- A 1988 Gallup Poll says that pharmacists and clergymen are the most trusted professionals, advertising people and car salesmen the least trusted.
- The United States is the fourth most populous nation in the world, ranking behind only China, India, and the Soviet Union.

- According to a *USA Today* poll, 66 percent of married women and 68 percent of married men have cheated sexually on their spouse.
- Over 100,000 refugees from Marxist Nicaragua live in Miami.
- No one has ever recovered from AIDS. The disease has a 100 percent mortality rate. Right now 1.5 million Americans are infected with AIDS. By the end of 1992, over 260,000 of them will be dead.

Note that there is a difference between factual statements and general assertions, such as you would make in a thesis or a major point. If you say:

"A free press is essential to a free society,"

you have made a general assertion (a conclusion, a claim), not a statement of fact. But, if you say:

"In 1690, the British colonial government suppressed the first American newspaper, *Publick Occurrences, Both Foreign and Domestic*, after only one issue,"

or

"By 1775 the 2.5 million Americans were served by 48 weekly newspapers,"

you have made a statement of fact. Your thesis and major points should be general assertions. Supporting material should be made up of facts. You can't prove a general assertion with another general assertion. Eventually, you must get to the facts. Once you have made a general assertion, you should prove it with facts.

The reason we've called this category of supporting material facts and *figures* is that simple factual statements are often more powerful if the facts are quantified in some way. To prove some statements you simply must count noses. If you want to convince your listeners that pornography is a widespread problem, it's not enough just to say "Too many people are exposed to smut!" Instead, tell them that with the advent of X-rated videos, Dial-A-Porn phone lines, and sexually explicit computer services, porn producers now do $10 billion worth of business each year. Tell them that a *Newsweek* survey revealed that 40 percent of all VCR owners polled admitted to buying or renting an X-rated videotape in the past year.

If you want your listeners to do something about pornography, don't just say their efforts will be effective. Tell them that from 1980 to 1987, public pressure on convenience stores (the primary source of sales) plunged the circulation of *Playboy* from 5 million to 3.4 million, and of *Penthouse* from 4.2 million to 2.2 million.

Figures can provide hard, quantifiable evidence for your case. Their one drawback is that statistics are often boring. Listeners will like your figures if and only if: (1) They are vital to your point; (2) they are easy to understand; and (3) they are properly visualized. Of those three rules, the last is most important. Your numbers must paint pictures.

For example, if you are talking about a billion dollars, a billion people, a billion miles, or a billion years, no one in your audience is going to have any practical comprehension of what those numbers mean. Though a billion of anything is a staggering amount, in order for that figure to impress an audience you must break it down into more comprehensible numbers. For example, you can bring a billion dollars closer to comprehension by breaking the sum into units of $1000 a day:

Suppose you owned a business that made you $1,000 a day. How long would it take you to earn a billion dollars? If you opened for business in the year A.D. 1 and earned $1,000 a day, you would not yet have earned a billion dollars when the Roman Empire ended over 400 years later. In fact, you would still be working at it when the Normans conquered England in 1066, when Columbus sailed from Spain in 1492, and when the U. S. Constitution was ratified in 1787. Even now you would have not yet earned a billion dollars. You would have to continue working, earning $1,000 a day, for another 748 years before you would have earned a billion dollars.

If you want to make a point on the growing tax bite that government takes out of our paychecks, *don't* do this:

In 1960 the IRS collected $91,774,8802,823 from 181 million Americans, or $507.96 per capita.

In 1970 the IRS collected $195,722,096,497 from 205 million Americans, or $955.31 per capita.

In 1980 the IRS collected $519,375,273,361 from 228 million Americans, or $2,275.66 per capita.

In 1988 the IRS collected $935,106,594,222 from 247 million Americans, or $3,792.15 per capita.

. . . . ZZZZZZZZZZZZZZZZZZZZZ . . . .

Instead, dress up those numbers by telling us about Tax Freedom Day:

Experts have devised a formula to calculate how long a person has to work to pay his taxes. Suppose you began paying your taxes for the year on January 1 and spent no money until they were paid in full. The day you finished paying your taxes and started paying for food, rent, clothes and the other necessities of life is called Tax Freedom Day.

In 1929, Tax Freedom Day fell on February 9. In 1940, it fell on March 8. In 1960, it fell on April 17. And in 1988, the average

American had to work from January 1 until May 4 just to pay his taxes![1]

Early in 1990, animal-rights advocates pushed for bans on the wearing of fur. In New York city, protesters besieged people wearing expensive furs, and the city of Aspen, Colorado, voted on an ordinance that, if passed, would have made Aspen the first furrier-free zone in America. Though the case for animal rights leaves me unconvinced, I was impressed with one fur-ban advocate's use of figures. The speaker pointed out that each year over 300 million animals are killed for their fur, 18 million of them in the United States. Those are remarkable numbers, but the speaker did better than that:

> If you have on a beaver coat, you are wearing 15 dead beavers.
> If you have on a fox coat, you are wearing 15 to 25 dead foxes.
> If you have on a mink coat, you are wearing 35 to 65 dead minks.
> If you have on an ocelot coat, you are wearing 12 to 25 dead ocelots.
> If you have on a tiger coat, you are wearing 3 to 10 dead tigers.

This speaker's use of statistics is good for two reasons. First, he breaks his numbers down into practical units we can visualize. Most of us have never seen 300 million of any kind of animal. But we can imagine twenty-five foxes or ten tigers. Second, the speaker joins these familiar numbers with the vivid idea of wearing dead animals. Thinking of your favorite winter coat as fur is one thing, but dead beavers is another matter.

Statistics are especially effective when coupled with a good story-form example. The story makes the numbers come alive and the statistics prove that the story is not an isolated case, but represents a quantifiable trend.

When you use statistics, dress them up. Give your listeners something that lets them see your numbers in their minds.

2. Story-Form Examples

An impatient Athenian crowd once hissed the orator Demosthenes, refusing to listen to him. Demosthenes quieted the crowd just long enough to announce that he had but a short story to tell them and then he would leave. He began: "A certain man hired an ass to go to Megara. At noon, when the sun was very hot, both the man who had hired the ass and the man who owned the ass wanted to sit in the shade created by the ass' shadow. The two began to shove each other aside. The owner insisted he had hired out the ass but not the shadow. The other insisted that since he had hired the ass, everything that belonged to the ass was his."

Demosthenes then turned as if to leave, but the crowd, intrigued by the story, would not allow him to leave. They insisted that he finish the story. Demosthenes turned to the crowd and asked, "How is it that you insist upon hearing the story of an ass' shadow, but will not attend to the great issues upon which I have come to speak?" At that, they permitted him to give his speech and the story of the ass' shadow remains unsolved to this day. Demosthenes knew the power a story has over an audience.

From *The Cat in the Hat* to "Days of Our Lives," all the world loves a story. Fables, legends, parables, adventures, sagas, tales, novels, chronicles, yarns. Good narratives of all kinds enchant the listener and rivet his attention to the speaker's voice. The first request most of us ever made as listeners was "tell me a story." The stories become more varied and sophisticated with age, but our fascination with them remains.

Jesus often used simple stories to teach important spiritual truths. The Gospels record fifty-two parables of Jesus. A story of two debtors teaches us to forgive as we have been forgiven. A lost sheep, a lost coin, and a lost boy show us the infinite value of a sinner to his Heavenly Father. Ten virgins waiting for a wedding party paint a vivid picture of our need to be always ready for the return of our Lord. Jesus, the master teacher, knew the power of stories.

Stories about famous people.—Listeners especially like stories that involve famous people. Take the *National Enquirer* for example. There's little chance the *Enquirer* is ever going to walk away with a Pulitzer prize in journalism. But that doesn't keep them from selling over four million papers every week. Why? The publishers of America's most widely read grocery-store tabloid know that most folks can't resist stories about famous people. Bill Cosby, Johnny Carson, Phil Donahue, Donald Trump, Ed McMahon, Mike Tyson, Jim Bakker. You'll meet whoever's hot in popular culture at the checkout stand on the cover of the *National Enquirer*. Though sensationalism is not a commendable quality in either a news journal or a speaker, making good use of human interest stories about people your audience knows is.

Stories that animate the pages of history.—Though history lectures rarely play to sell-out crowds, listeners do enjoy historical examples when they make people and events of the past come alive. They like stories that *animate* the pages of history. For example, a speech on the joy of giving could use this illustration:

On May 7, 1824, Beethoven made his last public appearance in Vienna. The packed house had gathered to hear the famous composer conduct his Ninth Symphony. At the conclusion of the Symphony, Beethoven continued to beat time to himself until Caroline Unger, a contralto soloist, took his arm and turned him around so that he could *see* the standing ovation of the crowd. Beethoven never *heard* the applause. He never even heard his own Symphony. He was stone deaf. He created and gave to the world a thing of great beauty that he himself could never experience.

Stories that animate the pages of sacred history can make a Bible lesson or sermon vivid and interesting. If you want us to understand the giving of the Ten Commandments, tell us a story that walks us from Egypt to Mount Sinai with the Israelites. Picture the mountain on the southern end of a granite ridge towering 7,000 above the desert floor. Tell how the sky grew dark as the wind blew and the earth quaked. Tell how the mountain smoked and burned with fire as God descended upon it.

Or, take us into the temple court in Jerusalem during the Feast of Tabernacles, while Jesus taught the people and confronted the scribes and Pharisees. Catch the drama of the scene as the Lord declared, "Before Abraham was born, I am!" and the Jews picked up stones to stone Him for blasphemy.

Seat us beside the apostle Paul, chained in the Mamertine Dungeon in Rome, as he writes his Second Letter to young Timothy in Ephesus. Help us catch the spirit of this great saint who faces his own execution at Nero's hand with this declaration: "I have fought the good fight, I have finished the race, I have kept the faith."

Historical examples are also helpful in problem-solving speeches. If you can offer your audience concrete examples of proven solutions to current problems, they are more likely to adopt them.

History is more than a dreary list of dates to memorize. It is a mine from which you can dig sparkling illustrations for speeches. Listeners like speakers who animate the adventures, sagas, and courageous deeds of great men and women from the past.

Hypothetical examples.—Don't overlook the power of stories from works of fiction or hypothetical examples you invent yourself. Hypothetical stories have taught some of the greatest lessons in history. After two and a half millennia, we remember a slave named Aesop and the morals taught by his fables. A hare and a tortoise teach us that "slow and steady wins the race." A fox who coaxes a goat into a well advises us to "look before you leap." A boy who cries wolf illustrates that "you cannot believe a liar even when he tells the truth."

When I was in the third grade, my teacher, Mrs. Wise (her real name), caught me flicking ink from a fountain pen onto a wall. She admonished me for two reasons. One, I should have known better in the first place, and, two, I had previously watched her punish another boy for the same act. Mrs. Wise exiled me to the corner of the room for the rest of the day. When school let out, she sat me down and told me one of Aesop's fables:

> A Lion, an Ass, and a Fox went out hunting together. They had soon taken a large catch of game, which the Lion asked the Ass to divide between them. When the Ass divided the game into three equal parts, the Lion was furious. He fell upon the Ass and tore him to pieces. Then, glaring at the Fox, the Lion asked him to make a

fresh division. The Fox gathered almost the whole into one great heap for the Lion's share, leaving only a few morsels for himself. "My dear friend," said the Lion, "who taught you to divide so well?" The Fox replied, "Mr. Ass." The moral of the story is: learn from the mistakes of others.

After thirty years, I remember this event and the lesson it taught because my teacher coupled it with a story.

Through his books, films, and popular radio broadcast *Focus on the Family*, Dr. James Dobson has given helpful advice to millions of parents. In making the point that anger is an ineffective method of controlling children, Dr. Dobson tells this hypothetical example:

Consider your own motivational system. Suppose you are driving your car over the speed limit. Standing on the corner is a lone policeman who has not been given the means to arrest you. He has no squad car, wears no badge, carries no gun, and can write no tickets.

All he can do is stand on the curb and scream threats at you. Would you slow down just because he shakes his fist in protest? His anger would achieve little except to make him appear foolish.

Nothing influences the way you drive more than looking in the rearview mirror and seeing a black and white vehicle in hot pursuit with red lights flashing. When you pull over, a dignified, courteous patrolman approaches your window.

"Sir," he says firmly but politely, "my radar indicates that you were traveling 65 in a 25-mile-per-hour zone." He opens his leatherbound book of citations and leans toward you. "May I see your driver's license please?" He has revealed no hostility and offers no criticisms.

But why are your hands moist and your mouth dry?

Why is your heart thumping in you throat? Because the *action* that the Law is about to take is notoriously unpleasant. Alas, it is that *action* that dramatically affects your future driving habits.

Disciplinary *action* influences behavior; anger does not.[2]

Specific instances.—Specific instances are condensed examples. If you are reasonably sure your audience is familiar with a certain story, person, or event, a simple mention of the instance, without a detailed explanation, may be enough to make your point.

Suppose you wanted to say that "great handicaps can be overcome." You could support that point with a series of specific instances:

Booker T. Washington was born in slavery. Thomas Edison was deaf. Abraham Lincoln's parents were illiterate. Lord Byron had a club foot. Robert Louis Stevenson had tuberculosis. Alexander Pope was a hunchback. Admiral Nelson had only one eye. Julius Caesar was an epileptic. Louis Pasteur was so nearsighted that he could not find his laboratory without his glasses. Helen Keller could neither see nor hear, but she graduated with honors from Radcliffe College. These people made history despite their limitations and disabilities. Great handicaps can be overcome![3]

Specific instances may stand alone, but, as in the above example, it is more effective to compound them. When the writer of Hebrews wanted first-century Jewish Christians to understand the idea of "faith," he used specific instances:

By faith Noah, when warned about things not yet seen, in holy fear built an ark to save his family. By his faith he condemned the world and became heir of the righteousness that comes by faith.

By faith Abraham, when called to go to a place he

would later receive as his inheritance, obeyed and went, even though he did not know where he was going. By faith he made his home in the promised land like a stranger in a foreign country; he lived in tents, as did Isaac and Jacob, who were heirs with him of the same promise.

By faith Joseph, when his end was near, spoke about the exodus of the Israelites from Egypt and gave instructions about his bones.

By faith Moses' parents hid him for three months after he was born, because they saw he was no ordinary child, and they were not afraid of the king's edict.

By faith Moses, when he had grown up, refused to be known as the son of Pharaoh's daughter. He chose to be mistreated along with the people of God rather than to enjoy the pleasures of sin for a short time.

By faith the people passed through the Red Sea as on dry land; but when the Egyptians tried to do so, they were drowned.

By faith the walls of Jericho fell, after the people had marched around them for seven days.

And what more shall I say? I do not have time to tell about Gideon, Barak, Samson, Jephthah, David, Samuel and the prophets, who through faith conquered kingdoms, administered justice, and gained what was promised; who shut the mouths of lions, quenched the fury of the flames, and escaped the edge of the sword; whose weakness was turned to strength; and who became powerful in battle and routed foreign armies (11:7-9,22-25, 29-30, 32-34).

Help your listeners see with their ears. Tell them stories about heroes and villains, about the people and events that changed the course of history. Take them to amazing sites and scenes, to great cities, and through vast wildernesses. Use story-form examples that paint specific, concrete images in your listeners' minds.

3. Analogies

An analogy points out similarities between an idea that is already known, understood, or believed by the listener, and one that is not. Graft the new idea that your audience doesn't understand or accept onto an old idea that they do.

C. S. Lewis was a master of the illustrative and argumentative use of analogies. My favorite Lewis analogy illustrates his argument against the philosophy of naturalism. Naturalism denies the existence of a rational, personal Creator. It says that the universe and everything in it, including us, is the result of the blind, irrational process of evolution. But if human beings are the result of irrational causes, then so is the human brain. If the human brain is the result of irrational causes, then so are human thoughts. If human thoughts are the result of irrational causes, then so is the philosophy of naturalism, which is the product of human thoughts. And, if the philosophy of naturalism is ultimately the product of irrational causes, why should we believe it to be true? Lewis's point is that a philosophy that discredits thinking cannot be true. The argument can be difficult to follow until Lewis illustrates it with a few apt analogies:

> To be the result of a series of mindless events is one thing: to be a kind of plan or true account of the laws according to which those mindless events happened is quite another. Thus the Gulf Stream produces all sorts of results: for instance, the temperature of the Irish Sea. What it does not produce is maps of the Gulf Stream. . . . It is as if cabbages, in addition to resulting *from* the laws

of botany also gave lectures in that subject: or as if, when I knocked out my pipe, the ashes arranged themselves into letters which read: "We are the ashes of a knocked-out pipe."[4]

Another Lewis analogy explains the change that must take place when a person becomes a Christian:

> The terrible thing, the almost impossible thing, is to hand over your whole self—all your wishes and precautions—to Christ. But it is far easier than what we are all trying to do instead. For what we are tying to do is to remain what we call "ourselves," to keep personal happiness as our great aim in life, and yet at the same time be "good." We are all trying to let our mind and heart go their own way—centered on money or pleasure or ambition—and hoping, in spite of this, to behave honestly and chastely and humbly. And that is exactly what Christ warned us you could not do. As He said, a thistle cannot produce figs. If I am a field that contains nothing but grass seed, I cannot produce wheat. Cutting the grass may keep it short: but I shall still produce grass and no wheat. If I want to produce wheat, the change must go deeper than the surface. I must be ploughed up and resown.[5]

Billy Graham makes apt use of an analogy in a sermon on the Bible:

> The Bible is the constitution of Christianity. Just as the United States Constitution is not of any private interpretation, neither is the Bible of any private interpretation. Just as the Constitution includes all who live under its stated domain, without exception, so the Bible includes all who live under its stated domain, without exception. As the Constitution is absolute, so the Bible is absolute. As the Constitution is the highest law of man, so the Bible is the highest law of God. God's laws

for the spiritual world are found in the Bible. Whatever else there may be that tells us of God, it is more clearly told in the Bible.[6]

W. Steven Brown, author of *Thirteen Fatal Errors Managers Make and How You Can Avoid Them*, says that one of the crucial errors managers make is to attempt to manage all their employees the same way. He illustrates the principle with an analogy:

> I hear frustrated managers declare a particular person a lost cause when a guy does not respond in exactly the same way another did to a particular technique. When one manager asked if I agreed that he should terminate a certain employee, I asked him to show me his key ring. Puzzled, he complied. I selected a key and asked, "What does this open?"
> "The door to my station wagon."
> "Will it also unlock your wife's car?"
> "No. Of course not."
> "Well, it's a perfectly good key. We know it works. Why don't you junk her car and get another one that will open with this station-wagon key?"
> Obviously he has another key that operates her car, just as another technique is the key to getting the second employee to respond in the desired way.[7]

4. Visual Aids

Of all the information stored in your mind, 87 percent of it entered through your eyes. Seeing is believing. When Shakespeare's character Othello questioned reports of his wife's infidelity he said, "Be sure of it; give me the ocular proof." Othello wanted proof he could see with his own eyes.

When the Pharisees attempted to trap Jesus by asking Him if it was right to pay taxes to Caesar, He called for a coin. They brought Him a denarius. Jesus asked, "Whose portrait is this? And whose inscription?"

"Caesar's," they replied.

Then He said, "Give to Caesar what is Caesar's, and to God what is God's." (Matt. 22:20-21).

Having no answer, His opponents left as the crowd stood amazed. A coin, a question, and a one-sentence reply. That's all. But it taught a lesson no one could forget.

I once had a student who spoke against a proposed state law to raise the weight limit on tractor-trailer trucks. She opened her speech by placing a small homemade ramp on a table top beside the podium and spreading a towel at the bottom of the ramp. From a paper bag she produced a cantaloupe and an egg. She held both of them up for the class to see and said: "The weight of this cantaloupe is roughly thirty times that of the egg."

She placed the egg at the bottom of the ramp, put the cantaloupe at the top, said "beep beep," and released the cantaloupe. The cantaloupe rolled down the ramp, smashed the egg, and kept on rolling. Since none of us had ever seen a cantaloupe run over an egg, the class roared with laughter. The speaker stepped behind the podium and said: "The average tractor-trailer truck outweighs the average passenger car thirty times over." She went on to show several slides of cars that had been smashed by trucks, just as the cantaloupe had smashed the egg. I've never forgotten the speech because of the vivid picture the speaker's visual aids planted in my mind.

In his last state of the union address, President Ronald Reagan called attention to the need to overhaul the federal budget process with a stunning visual aid. The

President noted that during his seven years in office, only ten out of ninety-one appropriations bills made it to his desk on time. With each missed budget deadline, Congress had to hurriedly pass a "continuing resolution" authorizing funds to keep the federal government from shutting down. In the fiscal year that had just ended, none of the thirteen appropriations bills due on October 1 had met the deadline. To make his point on the consequences of missing budget deadlines, the President actually produced the tower of paper needed to deal with the problem:

> This [the President said as he dropped a stack of papers onto the table beside the podium], this is the conference report, a 1,053 page report weighing 14 pounds. Then this [dropping another stack of papers], a reconciliation bill, six months late, that was 1,186 pages long, weighing 15 pounds. And the long-term continuing resolution [dropping a third stack], this one was two months late, and it's 1,057 pages long, weighing 14 pounds. Now, that was a total of 43 pounds of paper and ink. You had three hours, yes, three hours to consider each, and it took 300 people at my Office of Management and Budget just to read the bill so the government wouldn't shut down.[8]

If the President had simply said that Congress had made a mess of the federal budget process, we might have easily overlooked his point. But you can't ignore a speaker while he's dropping forty-three pounds of paper onto a table.

It may be a cliché, but often a picture really is worth a thousand words. Photographs, maps, posters, diagrams, graphs, models, exhibits, and other objects can powerfully enforce or clarify your point. Here are a few guidelines for using visual aids in your speeches:

1. Use your own audiovisual equipment or thoroughly check out the equipment you will use. The bulb on the projector will always go out the time you don't bother to bring a spare. To be effective, a piece of audiovisual equipment must be where you need it, when you need it, and must work the way you expect it to work.
2. Prepare for trouble. Have a back-up plan in case your equipment fails.
3. Face the audience. You lose your listeners when you turn your back on them and talk to the visual aid.
4. Make sure everyone in the room can see what you're showing them. Is the image large enough? Is it clear? Does each listener have an unobstructed view? Check it out.
5. Read every word on your chart, overhead, or slide to the audience. Your audience will read it whether you do or not. So, don't compete with your visual aids. Once you've read what's on the screen, you can comment or explain.
6. Don't overdo the visuals. One visual aid for each key point in your speech is enough.
7. Prepare handouts of all your charts, overheads, and slides that your listeners can keep. Tell them at the start that you will give them the handouts when you are through. This keeps them listening to you during the visuals, rather than taking notes, and gives them something to remember your speech by when they go home.
8. Rehearse with your visual aids. Go through your

complete presentation. You'll discover what needs to be shortened or reorganized.

As you look at the material in a speech, ask yourself "Which of my points could be explained or proven with visual aids? What images do I want the audience to remember?" Create those images with charts, overheads, slides, photographs, exhibits, or other visuals and you give your listeners a powerful reason to accept your speech.

5. Quotations

Quotations are like statistics. They can be great pieces of supporting material, but they must be used with care. You should use a quotation for one of two reasons: the wording of the quotation is so vivid and to the point that you can't think of another way to say it better; or the author has some expertise or authority you wish to marshal in support of your point.

Quotations that illustrate.—Does your speech need to make the point that the paths of earthly glory lead but to the grave? Tell your listeners the words of the Greek philosopher Diogenes when Alexander the Great asked why he was examining a heap of human bones. "I am searching for the bones of your father," Diogenes replied, "but I cannot distinguish them from those of his slaves."[9]

Do you want your listeners to seize an opportunity to launch out in some new endeavor? Tell them that Wayne Gretzky understands how to succeed by anticipating opportunities. Gretzky is the only professional hockey player to score more than fifty goals in fifty-or-fewer games in a single year. When an interviewer asked his secret, Gretzky replied, "I skate to where the puck is going to be, not where it has been."

Shakespeare is a dependable source for quotations on every subject. One of my favorite Shakespeare quotations illustrates how we, as recipients of God's grace, have a duty to be gracious to others. In *Measure for Measure*, Isabella is pleading for the life of her brother before an unsympathetic judge. The judge says: "Your brother is a forfeit of the law And you but waste your words." Isabella answers:

> Alas! alas! Why, all the souls that were were forfeit once; And He that might the vantage best have took, Found out the remedy. How would you be, if He, which is the top of judgment, should But judge you as you are? O! think on that, And mercy then will breathe within your lips, Like a man new made.[10]

The danger of a Christian allowing himself to be caught in sin after God has saved him can be illustrated with these lines from Shakespeare "The crow may bathe his coal-black wings in mire, and unperceived fly with the filth away, but if the like the snow-white swan desire, the stain upon his silver down will stay."[11]

Billy Graham used this quotation from Augustine to illustrate a point in a sermon: "Augustine had a motto printed on the wall of his dining room: 'He that speaks an evil word of an absent man or woman is not welcome at this table.' Would that we had this motto over every table in every home in America."[12]

Quotations like these add sparkle to your speech. The words of famous characters, framed in a short anecdotal background, have the same appeal as stories, which we discussed earlier.

Good poetry can also persuade and move an audience. A speech to inspire an audience to hard work in a worthy cause might use these lines from Longfellow:

> The heights by great men reached and kept
> Were not attained by sudden flight,
> But they, while their companions slept,
> Were toiling upward in the night.

Hymn texts are a useful source of inspiring poetry for speeches. A lesson on the unchangeable goodness of God finds eloquent confirmation in the words of a favorite hymn:

> Great is thy faithfulness, O God my Father,
> There is no shadow of turning with thee;
> Thou changest not, Thy compassion they fail not;
> As thou hast been Thou forever wilt be.[13]

Or, a challenge to Christian's to action in the cause of Christ could conclude with this:

> Rise up, O men of God!
> Have done with lesser things;
> Give heart and mind and soul and strength
> To serve the King of kings.
>
> Rise up, O men of God!
> The Church for you doth wait,
> Her strength unequal to her task;
> Rise up and make her great!
>
> Lift high the cross of Christ!
> Tread where His feet have trod;
> As brothers of the Son of Man,
> Rise up, O men of God![14]

The worlds of literature and hymnody are full of beautiful and inspiring verse to create within your listeners empathy and action for your cause. When using poetry, observe these guidelines:

1. Use only the good stuff. There is something particularly reprehensible about mediocre poetry.
2. Avoid too much poetry.
3. Avoid long poems.
4. Memorize and recite poems with feeling. Avoid reading poems.

Quotations that prove.—Besides their illustrative value, quotations can serve as proof for your point. The quoted observations, opinions, or testimony of an expert or an eyewitness can be very convincing.

For example, suppose you were speaking to defend the biblical doctrine of creation against the theory of evolution. You could make the point that one of the chief flaws of evolution is that the fossil record of how life began on earth does not portray a finely graduated chain of simple organisms evolving into more complex ones. Instead, the fossil record shows that the beginning of life on earth is marked by the sudden appearance of highly complex forms of life in great variety. To support that point, you could cite the following quotation:

In a recent college textbook entitled *The Science of Evolution*, William D. Stansfield, Professor of Biology at California Polytechnic University, said: "During the Cambrian Period there suddenly appeared representatives of nearly all the major groups of animals (phyla) now recognized. It was as if a giant curtain had been lifted to reveal a world teeming with life in fantastic diversity. The Cambrian 'curtain' has become the touchstone of the creation theory. Darwin was aware of the problem this created for evolutionists and it remains a problem today. Evolutionists keep hoping that new discoveries will eventually fill in the missing pieces of the fossil puzzle, but the chances of success may be less than those of

finding the proverbial 'needle in the haystack.' The great revolution that separates the Proterozoic (Pre-Cambrian) from the Pa-
leozoic eras apparently was of such a cataclysmic nature that
many of the earlier fossils were destroyed."

The missing fossils apparently were destroyed? Evolutionists
keep hoping they will be found? To the impartial observer, it is
apparent that an evolutionary explanation of the origin of life owes
more to imagination than to the hard evidence of the existing fossils. The most straightforward explanation of the evolutionists'
missing Pre-Cambrian fossils is that they never existed. Life on
earth did not evolve. It was created by God just as the Bible
says.[15]

When citing testimony to prove a point, you should:
name the author, state his qualifications, and name the
source of the quotation. It helps your listeners to know
that the evolution quotation didn't come from your
Aunt Edna's veterinarian, but from a distinguished
university professor of biology (whose words are on
page 76 of the textbook you cited, just in case someone
happens to challenge you).

Observe two precautions when using any kind of
quotations: keep them short; and use them sparingly.
Too many quotations will make the audience wonder
why you're giving the speech instead of the people
you're quoting.

6. Definitions and Descriptions

Definitions.—Sometimes your listener's chief need is
to *understand* what you're talking about. He needs a
definition. Dictionaries define terms by putting them in
a class, then distinguishing them from other things

that are also in that class. You can also define something by telling how it works, comparing and contrasting it with similar things, or by giving examples or synonyms. Tell what it looks, sounds, feels, smells, and tastes like.

Etymologies, or word histories, often make interesting speech illustrations. For example, the word *plagiarize*, meaning to steal and use ideas or writings of another as your own, comes from the Latin term *plagiarius*, a kidnapper. If you wouldn't dream of snatching someone's three-year-old off the street, then neither should you practice kidnapping other people's ideas, speeches, or writings.

Arguments on controversial issues often turn on the definition of important terms. For example, one of the central issues in the debate over legalized abortion is whether or not an unborn child is a living human being. Note how one speaker supports his position with a three-part definition:

Major Point: *From the moment of conception an unborn child is a living human being.*

A. An unborn child is *alive*.

● In 1965 *Life* magazine entitled an article on human conception "The Magic Moment When Life Begins."

● A 1970 editorial in *California Medicine*, the journal of the California Medical Association, admitted that even though they favored legalizing abortion, they were compelled to acknowledge "the scientific fact, which everyone knows, that human life begins at conception, and is continuous, whether intra or extrauterine, until death."

B. An unborn child is *human*.

● A basic law of genetics: like begets like. Dogs always have puppies; cats always kittens. Likewise, human beings are incapable of reproducing anything but other human beings.

● Dr. Clas Wirsen, in the best-seller on prenatal development, *A Child Is Born*, says: "When is it determined that we are going to be human beings? This happens at the moment of conception . . . for each species, growth is staked out from the beginning. Human genetic material can give rise only to human beings."

C. An unborn child is a unique *individual* and not simply an appendage of his mother's body.

● A 1979 article in the science section of the *New York Times* revealed that: "Even to your own mother, you are an immunological alien. She would almost certainly reject a skin graft from you, because part of you comes from your father, whose tissue is incompatible with hers. So why didn't she reject you as foreign tissue months before you were born?

"Researchers at the Blond McIndoe Transplant Research Center here have a startling answer: that soon after conception the fetus begins to aggressively repel its mother's immune attack. Their research forms part of a growing body of evidence that the fetus, at least immunologically, is not what it has always been thought—a defenseless creature totally dependent on its mother."

● Louise Brown, the world's first "Test-tube Baby," was conceived in a laboratory dish and spent the first three days of her life outside her mother's womb. Though she spent the next eight and a half months inside her mother's body, she was not a part of her mother, but a unique human individual.

● As early as eight to ten weeks after conception, an unborn child clearly *looks like a human baby*. (Show slides of early fetal development.)[16]

Descriptions.—A mail-order catalog describes a birdfeeder, a newspaper describes a house for sale, and a police circular describes a man wanted for kidnapping. In each case someone enumerates the details of a person or object for some practical purpose. The business people want to persuade someone to buy the articles described in their advertising. The police want someone to turn in a dangerous fugitive.

As a speaker you, too, must describe in order to persuade. You must give your audience both information and images. You must identify, define, and *describe* what you are talking about in a way that paints a mental picture in your listeners' minds.

For example, one of the great Scriptures on the meaning of the death of Jesus is 1 Peter 2:24: "He Himself bore our sins in His body on the cross, so that we might die to sin and live to righteousness" (NASB). A description of what a Roman crucifixion was like could give a congregation a greater appreciation of the truth Peter affirms in his epistle:

> When Scripture says Jesus bore our sins "in His body on the cross" it means that He did it here, on earth, in flesh and blood, in His own body as a man. This was no suspended sentence. Jesus literally carried it out in His own body.
>
> Arrested. Deprived of sleep. Lied about. Cursed. Spat upon. Mocked. Scourged. Crowned with thorns. And finally crucified.
>
> We must realize that the cross was not primarily an instrument of execution, but of torture. The Romans reserved it for traitors, military deserters, and the lowest of criminals. The condemned man was stripped naked to expose him to public shame and scorn. The Romans often nailed their victims to the cross in grotesque positions, contorting the body so as to cause muscle cramps. As fatigue set in, the pain from rigid, spasmodic contractions would be unbearable. A crucified man could suffer for as long as a week before dying of hunger, dehydration, exhaustion, exposure, shock, or suffocation. Crucifixion was a fate so horrible, the Gospel writers never describe it. They simply and reverently say: "they crucified him."
>
> The Lord Jesus deliberately submitted Himself to treatment as the worst of criminals, suffered in his own body the most shameful and painful form of death known to men, and came openly under the curse of God to save us from our sins and to make possible a new life for us in Him.[17]

How to Use Supporting Material

1. Make Frequent Use of Story-Form Examples

People love stories because abstract ideas are difficult to grasp. Most of the time we think in pictures. Theories of "beauty" mean nothing until you point to a flower or to the face of a child. You could speak for hours on the concept of "kindness" without enlightening your listeners as much as would a story of a teenager who sat with an elderly widow on her wedding anniversary.

Because people think in pictures, stories make the most effective kind of supporting material. If you animate the evidence in your speech with a narrative touch, no human ear will be able to resist it. Narrative examples interest and persuade because they paint pictures in your listeners' minds.

2. Supplement Your Story-Form Examples with Facts and Figures, Colorful Analogies, Visual Aids, Lively Quotations, Expert Testimony, or Definitions and Descriptions

Though story-form examples are the strongest kind of supporting material, sometimes they need help. A story about a five-year-old cocaine addict can be moving. But it doesn't establish whether that child is part of a national epidemic or only an isolated tragedy. To prove a larger trend, you would need to supplement the story with statistical evidence, expert testimony or other facts to prove that the point of that particular story is a general truth. Your speech will be more interesting and more believable if it uses a variety of supporting material.

3. Get Your Facts Straight

If you are narrating events to which you were a witness, tell precisely what you saw, heard, smelled, touched, or tasted. If your information comes secondhand, use a credible source.

The best guide for judging the credibility of a source is: does this person, journal, or institution have a reputation for getting their facts straight? Are they known for telling the truth? The difference between *U. S. News and World Report* and the *National Enquirer* is that one journal has a reputation for accuracy, the other for exaggeration. Choose sources that will, when known to your listeners, add credibility to your case.

Important points in your case should be confirmed by more than one source. The Romans had a legal maxim: "Testis unus, testis nullus." One witness equals no witness. Testimony that cannot be supported by other sources may prove as useless as no testimony at all. Your audience will be more likely to give credence to an example or statistic if you can confirm it with more than one source.

4. Stick to the Point

A speaker must not only get his facts right. He must get the *right* facts right. Each fact in your case must be directed to the matter at hand. It must be immediately obvious how each illustration, example, analogy, etc. supports the point you are making. Your listeners will not strain to see your meaning. *You* must make it clear.

5. Be Specific

In *The Excursions* Wordsworth said: "Give us, for our abstractions, solid facts; For our disputes, plain pictures."

We will talk more about being specific when we take up the matter of style in the next chapter. For now, as you consider supporting material for your speech, remember that specific facts are more interesting and more credible than generalities. In your examples make frequent use of names, dates, places, and detailed descriptions. Avoid abstract generalities. Tell your listeners who, what, where, when, how, and why.

6. Get as Close as You Can to Your Subject

In deciding legal issues, courts look for something called "best evidence." For example, a photocopy of a document may not be introduced as evidence if the original document is available. A deposition is not admissible if the witness who gave the deposition can be produced in court. All things being equal, best evidence is that which is most nearly immediate the event itself.

Primary sources are better than those that tell the story secondhand. Direct evidence is better than circumstantial evidence. Choose sources that put you as close as possible to your subject. Use best evidence.

7. Be Sure Your Evidence Is Strong Enough to Carry Your Point

There are degrees of proof. Every proposition will fall somewhere along this line of certainty: Impossible —> Possible —> Plausible —> Probable —> Certain.

Looking at your speech, do you have enough evidence and is the evidence you have strong enough to carry the points you're trying to make? For most points, you can tell a story or an analogy, cite a few relevant facts and figures and a good quotation, and your audience will be ready for you to move on. In some cases one good illustration can carry your point. In others, you will need more. How much evidence you will need to support a point is something you must decide case by case given the issue you are talking about and the degree of sympathy the audience has with your position on that issue.

8. Know Your Listeners

Dorothy and Toto want to get out of Oz and back to Kansas. The Scarecrow wants a brain. The Tin Man wants a heart. The Cowardly Lion wants courage. All four want to see the Wizard of Oz because they believe he can give them what they need. Your listeners, too, have special needs and interests. You must adapt your supporting material to your audience.

Who are your listeners? What do they already know about your topic? What do they know about you? What is their position on the issues in your speech? Do they have some reason to like or dislike you? What questions or objections are they likely to have? What is important to them? Who are your listeners in terms of age, sex, level of education, economic status, political affiliation, and, most importantly, their relationship with the Lord?

The better you know the people to whom you are speaking, the better you can adapt your material to their level of understanding, interests, and needs, and the better your chance of success. Remember Plato's observation that a speech is like a feast; it should be made to please the guests, not the cooks.

Summary

The business of a speech is to make and then make good a claim. Your speech must have both a *what* and a *why*. The thesis states the *what*. The body of your speech must give your listeners the evidence that provides the *why*. Remember these rules for selecting supporting material:

1. Make frequent use of story-form examples.
2. Supplement your story-form examples with facts and figures, colorful analogies, visual aids, lively quotations, expert testimony, or definitions and descriptions.
3. Get your facts straight.
4. Stick to the point.
5. Be specific.
6. Get as close as you can to your subject.
7. Be sure your evidence is strong enough to carry your point.
8. Know your listeners.

Notes

1. *The Universal Almanac 1990*, ed. John W. Wright (Kansas City: Andrews and McMeel, 1989), 141.
2. James Dobson, *Dr. Dobson's Focus on the Family Bulletin*, May 1990, 2.
3. C. Barry McCarty, "Who Is the Greatest?" sermon to the Cincinnati Bible College and Seminary Chapel, Feb. 27, 1990.
4. C. S. Lewis, "De Futilitate," *Christian Reflections* (Grand Rapids: William B. Eerdmans, 1967), 64-65.
5. C. S. Lewis, *Mere Christianity* (New York: Macmillan, 1943), 154.
6. Billy Graham, Sermon on "Our Bible," as cited in *The Wit and Wisdom of Billy Graham*, ed. Bill Adler (New York: Random House, 1967), 34-35.
7. W. Steven Brown, *Thirteen Fatal Errors Managers Make and How You Can Avoid Them* (New York: Berkley Publishing Co., 1987), 69.
8. Ronald Reagan, "State of the Union Address," *Vital Speeches*, February 15, 1988, 258-62.
9. *The Little, Brown Book of Anecdotes*, ed. Clifton Fadiman (Boston: Little, Brown and Co., 1985), xxi.

10. Act II, Scene 2.

11. *The Rape of Lucrece.*

12. Billy Graham, Sermon on "Things God Hates," as cited in *The Wit and Wisdom of Billy Graham,* ed. Bill Adler (New York: Random House, 1967), 117.

13. "Great Is Thy Faithfulness," Words by Thomas O. Chisholm, 1923, copyright 1923 by Hope Publishing Co., Carol Stream, Ill.; renewal 1951. All rights reserved.

14. "Rise Up, O Men of God," Words by William P. Merrill, 1911, copyright by *The Presbyterian Outlook,* Richmond, Va. All rights reserved.

15. C. Barry McCarty, "Scientific Objections to a Naturalistic Explanation of the Origin of the Universe," unpublished lecture notes, 1980.

16. C. Barry McCarty, "The Right to Life," speech to the Medical Student Association, University of Pittsburgh School of Medicine, May, 1979.

17. C. Barry McCarty, "Dying to Sin and Living for Righteousness," a sermon to the Cincinnati Bible College and Seminary Chapel, Nov. 10, 1989.

4

Style: Clothing Your Thoughts with Words

"How forcible are right words!"(Job 6:25, KJV).

"Style is the dress of thoughts, and well-dressed thought, like a well-dressed man, appears to great advantage." So said Lord Chesterfield.

Your style is how you express your thoughts in words. It is the way in which you say or write something. Because style is a personal quality, it is difficult to analyze. It is much like a frog. You can dissect the thing, but somehow it dies in the process. Though there is no single style of speaking that is best, there are some general principles that all good speaking styles share.

1. Speak to Great Issues

In *Measure for Measure*, Shakespeare's character the Duke of Vienna tells his young deputy Angelo: "Spirits are not finely touched but to fine issues." We have already discussed this principle in the first chapter on preparing speeches. It is worth repeating here in our discussion on style. The first step toward making a great speech is to have something worth saying. As the ancient rhetorician Longinus observed: "A great style is the natural outcome of weighty thoughts."

One of my favorite speeches is General Douglas MacArthur's farewell address to the Corps of Cadets at West Point in 1962, two years before his death. From the

Academy's motto, "Duty, honor, country," MacArthur fashioned an eloquent call to these young soldiers to commit themselves to the code of conduct and chivalry embodied in their motto:

> Duty, honor, country: Those three hallowed words reverently dictate what you ought to be, what you can be, what you will be. They are your rallying point to build courage when courage seems to fail, to regain faith when there seems to be little cause for faith, to create hope when hope becomes forlorn. . . .

Throughout the speech, MacArthur described the American soldier who throughout the nation's history has lived and died by that code:

> In twenty campaigns, on a hundred battlefields, around a thousand campfires, I have witnessed that enduring fortitude, that patriotic self-abnegation, and that invincible determination which have carved his statue in the hearts of his people.
>
> From one end of the world to the other, he has drained deep the chalice of courage. As I listened to those songs [of the Cadet Glee Club], in memory's eye I could see those staggering columns of the First World War, bending under soggy packs on many a weary march, from dripping dusk to drizzling dawn, slogging ankle-deep through the mire of shell-pocked roads; to form grimly for the attack, blue-lipped, covered with sludge and mud, chilled by the wind and rain, driving home to their objective, and, for many, to the judgement seat of God.
>
> I do not know the dignity of their birth, but I do know the glory of their death. They died, unquestioning, uncomplaining, with faith in their hearts, and on their lips the hope that we would go on to victory. Always for them: Duty, honor, country. . . .

Toward the end of the address, the General concluded with a sober warning:

> From your ranks come the great captains who hold the nation's destiny in their hands the moment the war tocsin sounds. The long grey line has never failed us. Were you to do so, a million ghosts in olive drab, in brown khaki, in blue and grey, would rise from their white crosses, thundering those magic words: Duty, honor, country. [1]

These short passages do not do the speech justice. As a study in how great issues and ideas lend themselves to great speeches, the speech is worth reading in its entirety. The power of MacArthur's address comes from powerful ideas. Patriotism, commitment to a noble cause, self-sacrifice, duty, honor, country—these are great issues. And great speeches start with great issues.

Discipline your mind to think great thoughts. Truth, justice, liberty, compassion, the great ideas cannot be strangers to the thoughts and words of one who would lead others through his speeches.

2. Paint a Picture for Your Listeners

There is an Arab proverb that says "he is a good speaker who can turn an ear into an eye." Good speakers use words as artists use brushes and paint. If you would persuade, portray. Don't merely present a truth; picture it.

The Scripture says that the common people heard Jesus gladly. They had good reason. The Lord didn't talk about the obligations of the law of Moses imposed by the teaching of the rabbis. He spoke of "heavy burdens and grievous to be borne, on men's shoulders" (Matt. 23:4, KJV). He didn't talk about a pharisaical doctrine of salvation so demanding that none could achieve it, not even those who taught it. He said, "Ye shut up the kingdom of heaven against men: . . . neither go in yourselves, neither suffer ye them that are entering to go in" (v.13). He didn't say the Jews' money-lending practices were so harsh that people who mortgaged their property were sure eventually to lose it. He said, "Ye devour widows' houses" (v.14). He didn't say they gave too much attention to keeping the external requirements of the law while ignoring the motives in their hearts. He said, "Woe unto you, scribes and Pharisees, hypocrites! for ye are like unto whited sepulchers, which indeed appear beautiful outward, but are within full of dead men's bones, and of all uncleanness" (v.27). When Jesus spoke He talked of bursting wineskins, playing children dressed up for weddings, a king taking account of his servants, or an enemy sowing weeds among a man's wheat.

Jesus talked in images that He projected onto mental screens. He painted pictures. And no one ever found Him boring. If we would speak and teach with power, we must do as He did. We must constantly picture the truth in vivid images.

The Scottish-born preacher Peter Marshall also painted vivid images with his sermons. During World War II, Marshall was minister of the New York Avenue Church in Washington, D.C., and chaplain of the United States Senate. His eloquent diction, imagination, and ability to dramatically portray the people and events of Scripture have seen few equals. Some of his sermons are still available on audio tape. It would be worth your while to listen to and study his preaching style. In the following portion of Marshall's sermon "Trumpet of the

Morn," he describes the scene as Peter denies Christ. Listen:

> Then a soldier who had just come out of the palace joined the group around the fire. As he greeted his friends in the circle his eyes fell on Peter. He looked him over very carefully and Peter, feeling this scrutiny of the newcomer, looked round as the soldier asked, "Did not I see thee in the garden with Him?" jerking his head in the direction of the palace. And another man chimed in, "Why certainly he must be one of the Galileans, his speech betrayeth him. Listen to his accent." And the soldier stubbornly went on, "I'm sure I saw him in the garden for my kinsman, Malchus, you know, was wounded by one of them who drew a sword. And if I'm not mistaken, it was this very fellow." And then Peter began to bluster. He denied. He used language he had not used for three years. It was vile language. He shouted, "I tell you I know not the man!" Why, they were shocked at his vehemence. They looked at him in amazement. But it was his face that startled them because it was livid, it was distorted. His eyes were blazing and his mouth was snarling like a cornered animal.
>
> It was a shocked silence. A silence so intense that the crowing of a distant cock somewhere sounded like a bugle call. And immediately Peter remembered Christ's prophecy. "Before the cock crows twice, thou shalt deny me thrice." He caught his breath. His face flushed. Hot tears came to his eyes. He turned away from the fire and through the mist of tears he saw ahead some movement on the stairs that led to Pilate's palace. For it was just at that moment that Christ was being led from the high priest to appear before Pilate. The Lord had heard. He had heard every hot, searing word. He had heard every blistering denial, the foul, filthy fisherman's oaths. He had heard them all.[2]

The preaching of Peter Marshall exemplifies many rules of good style. His words are simple, clear, specific, and imaginative. But, most of all, his language appeals to the listener's senses. He paints such vivid pictures that we see what he says.

Garrison Keillor is another speaker and writer who is worth careful study. Keillor is best known as the host of "A Prairie Home Companion," heard weekly on radio from 1974 to 1987. His weekly stories about his fictional hometown, Lake Woebegon, are stylistic masterpieces. In one story, Keillor, tells about meeting a retarded childhood friend he had not seen for twenty years. Listen as he paints the scene:

> I think of a boy I went to grade school with. His name was Donny Hart. The Harts lived in Lake Woebegon for only about four years. They were a kind of secretive family. They kept to themselves, at least that was how we saw it. So we mainly just knew their boy, who was a large boy and was much bigger than the rest of us in the grade school. He was, I suppose, about five and a half feet tall and was rather heavy. He had a thatch of black hair, and he spent all four years in the fifth grade. He was "held back" in the grades because, as we said at the time, "he was slow." . . .
>
> We hung around together for several years in grade school and the more I hung around with him, the more, even though I didn't mean to, I enjoyed his company. Because unlike other children, he was not competitive and when you were with him he simply enjoyed your company and never was interested in having any sort of advantage. He was a sweet person. Had a sweet disposition. And I missed him when they left town.
>
> And then I didn't think about him anymore until I saw him again, twenty years later. . . .[3]

Though Garrison Keillor no longer does a weekly broadcast, recordings of his Lake Woebegon stories are still available. The stories also continue in his books *Lake Woebegon Days, Leaving Home,* and *We Are Still Married.*[4] He is worth reading and hearing.

Great speakers like Peter Marshall and Garrison Keillor have a facility for picturesque speech. They attract and hold audiences by creating images in their own minds, then selecting the words that will transfer those images to the minds of their listeners.

When you speak, remember that your listeners' brains lie behind their eyes as well as between their ears. The words you speak last only for a moment. But the images they conjure up in the mind can remain for a lifetime. When you speak, you must portray before the eyes of your hearers a living image of the truth you would have them embrace and act upon. Develop and exercise your powers of diction and imagination. Let your audience see what you say. Paint them a picture.

3. Be Specific

Peggy Noonan, who worked as a speechwriter for Presidents Reagan and Bush, talks about making a speech for President Reagan's 1984 China trip more interesting:

> The State Department draft for [the speech to students at Fudan University] was just fine and a little boring. It's not interesting to say, "America loves freedom," it's interesting to say, "Freedom to us is newspapers that everyone can buy on the street corner, newspapers that get to say just about anything about anybody—including me [the President], and I'm supposedly the top man . . . Freedom to us . . ." and so on. Be specific, personalize. Make it real.[5]

In a sermon on "Confusing Good with Evil," Billy Graham uses specific details to describe how liquor advertisements entice people to drink:

> What is more beautiful than the full-page, full-color ads of "the man of distinction," dressed impeccably, sipping a glass of whiskey with his friends in the warmth of a well-appointed room? These ads say nothing of the new alcoholics that are being made every day, nor of the growing problem of excessive drinking that is eating at the heart of our civilization. Of course, it wouldn't be good taste to show a picture of a "man of distinction" on skid row, who began his drinking on Fifth Avenue but is ending it in the Bowery. It wouldn't be in good taste, but it would be honest. "Woe unto them that call evil good!"[6]

If you want a style that makes people sit up and listen, be specific. Show your listeners what you are talking about in specific, accurate, and evocative details. Don't attempt to make your point with abstract generalities. Describe concrete things in the real world.

For example, which is more interesting: *He passed between two trees*, or *He passed between a tall pine and a large oak*? The second sentence creates more of a picture in the mind. The specific is always more interesting. Specific words are also more accurate.

Are you more moved to learn that *many children are victims of sexual abuse*, or that *one of every four girls in the United States will be sexually molested before she turns eighteen*?

Does the word *produce* make your mouth water? What about *a Red Delicious apple* or *a tree-ripened orange*?

Are you more frightened at the thought of an *assailant with a formidable weapon* or *a large, dirty man who came at us with a heavy lead pipe*?

Which statement alarms you: "There's a lot of pollution in major cities" or "People who live in New York, Detroit, and Los Angeles breathe unsafe air an average of thirty-five days per year"?

Don't say a *long time ago, in the near future,* or *a lot of flowers.* Say *in October of 1066, two weeks from tomorrow,* or *500 yellow roses.* Don't say *The man went down the road.* Say he *stumbled, darted, pranced, trotted, skipped, shuffled, crawled,* or *slinked.* Contrast "My husband is dead," she *said* with " 'My husband is dead!' she *shouted.*" Or *blurted, cried, whispered, mumbled, ranted,* or *sobbed.*

Beware of generic adjectives that need the help of adverbs or other adjectives to do the job. For example, any adjective that needs a *very* to bring it up to speed is probably too weak to start with. Look for a more specific word. Don't say the water was *very hot.* Say it was *scalding.* Don't say it was *not very hot.* Say it was *lukewarm* or *tepid.* A *very hot* day can be *scorching, broiling, blistering,* or *sizzling.* A *very hot and humid* day can be *sweltering, stifling,* or *sultry.* Don't say the man was *very angry.* Tell us he was *furious.* Don't say something was *very large.* Say it was *huge, immense, tremendous, vast, colossal, monstrous, whopping, enormous,* or *massive.*

4. Use Strong Nouns and Verbs

Nouns and verbs, not their assistants, give good speaking its strength and color. Don't pile on modifiers to bolster weak nouns and verbs. Choose strong nouns and verbs to start with. For example, notice how the

Bible tells the great drama of creation with nouns and verbs and few adjectives:

> In the beginning God created the heaven and the earth.
> And the earth was without form, and void; and darkness was upon the face of the deep. And the Spirit of God moved upon the face of the waters.
> And God said, Let there be light: and there was light.
> And God saw the light, that it was good: and God divided the light from the darkness.
> And God called the light Day, and the darkness he called Night. And the evening and the morning were the first day (Gen. 1:1-5, KJV).

Let your nouns and verbs do the work. Don't say Shadrach, Meshach, and Abednego were *quickly and forcibly placed into* the fiery furnace. Say the guards *thrust* or *hurled* them into it. Don't tell a sinner that Christ is waiting to *eagerly and immediately make him safe* from eternal perdition. Tell him the Lord stands ready to *snatch* him from the fires of hell. Don't say the streets of heaven will *be very shiny*. Say they will *sparkle*.

E. B. White was right: "The adjective hasn't been built that can pull a weak or inaccurate noun out of a tight place."[7]

5. Use Imaginative Words

There are two ways to paint pictures in your listeners' minds: literally and figuratively. We have already discussed painting word pictures with stories and descriptions. Good speakers also paint pictures with imaginative figures of speech, such as similes, metaphors, and hyperboles.

A simile is a comparison between two essentially unlike things based on a shared characteristic. They are introduced by the words *like* or *as*. Metaphors are compressed similes. The words *like* or *as* are omitted. Instead of saying one thing is like another, a metaphor says it is another. Hyperbole is exaggeration for the sake of emphasis. Metaphors, similes, hyperboles, and other figures of speech create vivid comparisons and contrasts that help your listeners understand, picture, and, sometimes, even feel your ideas.

For example, Jesus used many similes to explain spiritual truths about His kingdom: "The kingdom of heaven is like leaven . . . a grain of mustard seed . . . treasure hid in a field . . . a man which built an house . . . a net that was cast into the sea . . . a merchant man, seeking goodly pearls . . . a man which sowed good seed in his field." Jesus often described Himself in metaphors: "I am the Good Shepherd . . . the light of the world . . . the door to the sheep fold."

Reading good fiction is a source of imaginative comparisons and figures of speech. Garrison Keillor gives us an imaginative simile in his *Lake Woebegon Days*: "I grew up among slow talkers, men in particular, who dropped words a few at a time like beans in a hill."[8] Another simile describes how parents keep children quiet in church: "When I was a kid, we sat quietly on Sunday morning sometimes for forty or fifty seconds at a stretch. Fidgety kids were put between two grownups, usually your parents or sometimes a large aunt. Like tying a boat to a dock."[9]

Keillor is also a master of hyperbole. Picture his description of a fresh tomato: "Not the imported store tomatoes that were strip-mined in Texas, but fresh garden tomatoes that taste like tomatoes."[10] Though only a small town, Lake Woebegon put on a Memorial Day parade of such proportions that: "They could add two senators and an elephant and it wouldn't be any more magnificent than it is."[11] Keillor portrays the honesty of one of his characters with this exaggerated testimonial: "Clarence Bunsen said that Roman Winkler could not be convicted of horse theft anywhere in Mist County if they found the horses in his bedroom."[12] And Florian Krebsbach was a man of such pure speech that: "you couldn't get a swear word out of him if you squeezed him with a pair of pliers."[13] Finally, on people who talk slowly, Keillor offers: "My Uncle Emmett has some unfinished sentences that go back to the Hoover Administration."[14]

In his *Prince of Tides*, Pat Conroy describes, with this simile, a gifted young writer giving her high school valedictory address: "It was the poet going public for the first time, cocky with the majesty of words that she used like a peacock fanning his gorgeous tail feathers for the sheer joy of ostentation."[15] Another simile portrays an affectionate grandmother doting on her grandchildren: "She kissed us until we purred like cats."[16] Later, Conroy links metaphor and simile to paint a moving picture of the grandmother's final days:

> My grandmother, Tolitha Wingo, is now dying in a Charleston nursing home. Her mind, as they say, is wandering a bit, but she still has rare moments of perfect clarity when one can glimpse the full, illuminate personality that her advancing age has veiled with a shroud of senility. The capillaries of her brain seem to be drying up slowly, like the feeder creeks of an endangered river.[17]

C. S. Lewis often used fresh figures of speech to explain difficult theological truths. This example is from *The Problem of Pain*:

> We can rest contentedly in our sins and in our stupidities; and anyone who has watched gluttons shoveling down the most exquisite foods as if they did not know what they were eating, will admit that we can ignore even pleasure. But pain insists upon being attended to. God whispers to us in our pleasures, speaks in our conscience, but shouts in our pains: it is His megaphone to rouse a deaf world. . . . No doubt pain as God's megaphone is a terrible instrument; it may lead to final and unrepentant rebellion. But it gives the only opportunity the bad man can have for amendment. It removes the veil; it plants the flag of truth within the fortress of a rebel soul.[18]

Fresh, lively figures of speech add color, warmth, and emotional power to your speech. Your listeners want you to paint a picture for them. That picture may be literal, as in a historical example, or it may be figurative, as in a metaphor or simile. Look for and learn to create imaginative word pictures with figures of speech.

6. Use the Active Voice

Passive verbs suck the life out of your sentences. They hide the actor behind the action or the object or both. Compare "worms are eaten by birds" or "decisions are made by men" with "birds eat worms" and "men make decisions." Passive constructions use more words and are less direct. A simple sentence in the active voice tells your listeners plainly who is doing what to whom. Passives work only when you have good reason to highlight the person or thing that is acted upon.

Above all, avoid the buck-passing passives that speak

of deeds without doers. In an address on current problems in public education, don't say: "Much recent discussion has focused upon the problem of illiteracy in America." Tell us that "Parents from Portland to Philadelphia are asking why their children cannot read or write." Don't say: "The haphazard application of disciplinary action must be eliminated." Say that "People who discipline children ought to be consistent."

In his delightful book *The Graves of Academe*, Richard Mitchell exposes examples of jargon, faulty syntax, redundancy, and other outrages against English committed by professional educators. One of Mitchell's targets is the statement of a professor of education who declared that, "The pre-school years have been recognized as being important formulative years." Mitchell notes that the speaker escapes having to actually say that the preschool years *are* formulative by using the passive voice (*have been recognized*).

> It matters not at all to the "professional" that what he has to say is obvious and banal and widely enough known that it needs no saying; he still finds a way to evade responsibility for having said it. In this timid language of misdirection and abdication, no one would dare stand forth and proclaim that a turkey is a turkey. He might mutter, tentatively, that a turkey has been recognized as being a turkey—although not necessarily by *him*.[19]

Don't use buck-passing or lifeless passives. Get the actor out front. Have the birds eat the worms. Use the active voice.

7. Watch Your Grammar

If you're Jerry Clower or Minnie Pearl, ignoring the conventions of traditional grammar is part of your charm. For the rest of us, a good speaking style starts with good grammar. Like it or not, people will judge you by your ability to use language correctly.

As a public speaker, your grammar should be informal, but not illiterate. Your listeners are not interested in hearing a prissy know-it-all who is compelled to demonstrate his mastery of the subjunctive mood every time he rises to speak. But neither will they put much stock in an ignorant, unsophisticated speaker who "don't know them there rules of grammar too good." Your listeners want to hear the informal, conversational speech of an educated, literate adult. They want cultivated colloquial speech.

In a speech, the average listener will neither notice nor care if you say *will* when you should have said *shall*, or *who* when you should have said *whom*. The following rules are a few of the basic conventions of grammar that you must observe. Violating these standards will mark you as a speaker of little linguistic sophistication. Check your grammar to be sure you understand and observe the following rules.

Make your subjects and verbs agree.—Singular subjects take singular verbs. Plural subjects take plural verbs. For example, in the sentence "The *plate looks* hot" the singular subject, *plate*, takes the singular form of the verb *to look*, *looks*. But if the subject is plural it takes the plural form of the verb: "The *plates look* hot." One *is*, but two *are*. One *was*, but two *were*. One *has*, but two *have*. One *goes*, but two *go*.

Subjects joined by *and* are usually plural and require

a plural verb. "The Old *and* New Testaments *are* the word of God." The exception is two singular subjects that refer to the same thing. "My Lord *and* Master *is* Jesus Christ." Singular subjects joined by *or* or *nor* are usually singular. "Either heaven *or* hell *awaits* every man."

Do not be misled by words that come between your subject and verb. "The *history* of the ancient Egyptians and Babylonians *testifies* to the accuracy of the Old Testament Scriptures." I once heard a sermon by a television evangelist on the subject "Which Church Is the Right Church." He opened the sermon by holding up a telephone book and reading the names of different churches in the city where he was preaching. After a dozen names or so, he held the phone book aloft and asked "Which of these churches are the right church?" Hmm. Perhaps the Baptist church are the right church. Maybe the Church of Christ are the right church. Or, maybe some other church are it. The speaker's problem is that he mistook the plural noun *churches* for the subject of his sentence. The real subject is *which*, which in this case is singular. Pay attention to your subjects and verbs. Always make them agree in number.

Use appropriate verb forms.—The English language has more than thirty verb tenses. To begin with, we have past, present, and future: I *see*, I *saw*, I *will see*. Then we have the present perfect, I *have seen*, the past perfect, I *had seen*, and the future perfect, I *will have seen*. Each of these tenses also has a progressive form: I *was seeing*, I *am seeing*, I *will be seeing*, I *have been seeing*, I *had been seeing*, and I *will have been seeing*. There is more, but we'll stop here.

Most of the time literate adults have no trouble using

the correct verb tense. There are, however, a few irregular verbs that can be trouble. Here are some of the most often misused verbs and their correct forms:

Present Tense	Past Tense	Past Participle
begin	began	has begun
break	broke	has broken
choose	chose	has chosen
drink	drank	has drunk
eat	ate	has eaten
lay	laid	has laid
lie	lay	has lain
rise	rose	has risen
shrink	shrank	has shrunk
spring	sprang	has sprung
swim	swam	has swum

A good college-level dictionary will give you the principal parts of all verbs. For example, the *American Heritage Dictionary* gives the present tense, the past tense, the past participle, the present participle, and the third-person singular present tense for every verb. Under the verb *know*, the dictionary has *knew, known, knowing,* and *knows*. If you don't know the proper form for a particular verb, look it up in the dictionary.

Make your pronouns agree with their antecedents.— Just as subjects and verbs should agree in number, so should pronouns and the nouns to which they refer. For example, in the sentence "*Each* of the churches had *its* own missions offering," *each* is the antecedent of *its*. Both are singular. "Each of the churches had *their* own missions offering" is incorrect.

Two or more antecedents joined by *and* use a plural

pronoun. "My mother *and* father celebrated *their* fifti-eth wedding anniversary this year." Singular anteced-ents joined by *or* or *nor* use a singular pronoun. "Nei-ther *Peter nor John* lost *his* boldness when confronted by the court." Collective nouns use a singular pronoun when they refer to the group as a whole and use a plural pronoun when they refer to individuals or parts of the group. "Our church's *choir is* writing *its* own music [not *their* own music]." Or, "Our *deacons do* not always agree on methods, but *they* are united on our mission."

Keep your adjectives and adverbs straight.—Adjec-tives modify nouns and pronouns. Adverbs modify verbs, adjectives, and other adverbs. Don't use an adjec-tive for an adverb. Don't say "They sang it *perfect*," but "They sang it *perfectly*." Don't say "He spoke *real good*," but "He spoke *well*." When in doubt, consult a dictionary. The part-of-speech label at each entry will tell you whether a word is an adjective, an adverb, or another part of speech.

Do not use double comparisons.—*Slower* means *more slow*. Thus, you should not say "They should drive *more slower*," but simply "They should drive *slower*." Don't say "He wants to speak *more better*," but "He wants to speak *better*."

Do not use double negatives.—Double negatives are a pattern of speech from the basement level of grammar. Avoid them. "I don't see *no* books on the shelf," "The door *won't* open *no* more," and "She *don't* live here *no* more," are all obviously illiterate forms of speech. Try "I don't see *any* books on the shelf," "The door *won't* open *any*more," or "She *doesn't* live here *any*more."

Breaking bad habits of grammar.—What should you do if you have problems keeping any of the basic rules of grammar we discussed above? Norman Lewis, author of *Better English*, offers a good method.[20] Since basic patterns of grammar are habitual, you must develop an acute awareness of your faults to correct them. For each unacceptable pattern prepare two small index cards containing both the objectionable phrase and the acceptable alternative. Like this:

> doesn't   any
>
> She ~~don't~~ work here ~~no~~ more.

Put one card in your wallet next to your money. Put the other on the bathroom mirror or in another place where you will see it the first thing each morning. The cards will remind you several times each day that you are trying to rid yourself of errors in your speech.

If you lack confidence in your grammar, you should also take a good college-level course in basic English. If you've never had a good course or if you had one but didn't do very well, enroll in a class at a college or university near you or look for a good college correspondence course. One caution: make sure the course you sign up for will give you a good dose of old-fashioned, nuts and bolts, prescriptive, grammar. The last thing you need is a modern, clarify-your-values, get-in-touch-with-your-feelings, creative English class.

The secret to correct grammar when you speak.—The best way to keep your speech grammatical is to *use short sentences.* Most literate adults have little trouble with the grammar of short sentences. But the more words you stuff into a sentence, the harder it is to keep up with them. There is plenty of room in a long sentence to mismatch a plural subject with a singular verb, dangle a modifier, or leave a shapeless parenthetical remark hanging in the air. Don't let your sentences crumble under their own weight. Use plenty of periods. Keep your sentences short.

8. Avoid Word Wax

In ancient Rome unscrupulous sculptors would hide flaws in a statue by putting beeswax into cracks. The purchaser would not discover he had a flawed statue until it was too late. To distinguish their work, reputable sculptors labeled their work *sine cera*, which is Latin for *without wax*. The phrase is the root of our English word *sincere*.

In public speaking *word wax* is anything that weakens, obscures, or is not a vital part of the thought you seek to express.[21] Here are a few kinds of word wax that you should avoid:

Clichés.—A cliché is a phrase, metaphor, or expression that has been worn out by overuse. There is no such thing as an exhaustive list of clichés, but this sample will do for starters:

- last but not least
- black as coal (or tar)
- bold as a lion
- bright as the sun
- clean as a whistle
- clear as crystal
- cool as a cucumber
- dark as night

- dead as a doornail
- dry as a bone
- easy come, easy go
- fit as a fiddle
- flat as a pancake
- free as a bird
- fresh as a daisy
- good as gold
- grin like a Cheshire cat
- hard as a rock
- honest as the day is long
- light as a feather
- mad as a hatter
- nervous as a cat
- old as the hills
- pretty as a picture
- quiet as a mouse
- red as a rose
- shake like a leaf
- sharp as a razor
- thin as a rail.
- fell like a ton of bricks
- ugly as sin
- white as a sheet

James J. Kilpatrick describes clichés as "poor, tired, but comfortable and familiar cubbyholes to which we retreat when imagination fails us. . . . They fall like casual dandruff on the fabric of our prose. They are weary, stale, flat, and unprofitable."[22]

Clichés mark you as a lazy, thoughtless, unimaginative speaker. If you use stale, trite, hackneyed expressions, then you become stale, trite, and hackneyed. Look for new ways of seeing and saying things. Enlarge your vocabulary. Keep a list of new words and phrases to use in your speeches. Keep another list of tired, trite expressions that need fresh images to take their place. Avoid clichés.

Superlatives.—If the facts themselves do not make the listener's pulse beat faster, it is not your place to spur and whip him into a contrived state of excitement. Don't say something is the *most*, the *first*, or the *only one of its kind* unless you know good and well that it is.

Be careful with words like *provocative, brilliant, historic, crucial,* or *crushing.* Beware of applying words such as *drastic* to price cuts at a J. C. Penney white sale. Amputating a gangrenous leg to save a patient's life is a *drastic* measure.

Avoid false superlatives and comparatives. Things that are absolute cannot be modified or compared. For example: "This is absolutely and positively essential!" or "This is true beyond any possible shadow of a doubt." If something is essential, it is essential. You cannot do without it. There are no degrees of comparison. Something is either essential or it is not. If something is true, it's true. There are no helping words that can make it more or less so.

Make sure there is substance in your speech. Use strong nouns and verbs to express strong ideas. Avoid weak words and ideas that would tempt you to use superlatives you don't need.

Qualifiers.—A qualifier takes a clear, decisive statement and weakens it. "Well, *it's only my opinion,* but . . . ." "I think that *maybe.* . . ." "It was *sort of* . . . ." Qualifiers are leeches that infest the pond of speech. Attach them to a plain statement and they'll suck the life right out of it. The speaker who says "I'm *pretty* sure about this" isn't sure about anything. A point that is *more or less, kind of, fairly, rather,* or *somewhat* important is no such thing. Don't let qualifiers mark you as a speaker who is afraid to make a decision or take a stand. Don't let these weasel words rob your speech of power. Do your homework. Know your facts. Stake out a position and plainly tell your listeners where you stand. Avoid qualifiers.

Euphemisms.—A euphemism is the substitution of a mild or vague expression for a blunt or disagreeable one. Euphemisms turn the *town drunk* into a *public inebriate,* an act of *adultery* into an *extramarital relationship,* or a *slum* into a *culturally deprived environment.* Though a speaker should not be coarse or crude, he should politely call things by their right names.

Euphemisms take the edge off your language and weaken the images conveyed by plain words. *Perspire* is a weak word. *Sweat* is a strong one. *Expectorate* is feeble. *Spit* is forceful. *Indicate* is wimpy. *Say* is plain. When real men have to sweat, they sweat; when they have to spit, they spit; and when they have something to say, they don't indicate, they say it.

Don't tell us the man was *discharged from his position.* Tell us he was *fired.* Don't say the witness uttered a *prevarication,* a *categorical inaccuracy,* or a *terminological inexactitude.* Tell us he *lied.* Don't tell us we can *exercise an option.* Tell us we can *choose.* Use plain language. Avoid euphemisms.

Jargon.—The technical vocabulary of a science, art, trade, profession, or class is called *jargon.* Technical language is fine when confined to its own context. But jargon confuses and alienates people who don't use it every day. The Army might know what a *combat emplacement evacuator* is, but the rest of us need to hear the word *shovel*. A sociologist might describe an *unstructured conversational interaction*. The rest of us would say that Betty dropped by for a *chat*. If you're talking to people who manage businesses, they'll know what you mean by *fixed costs, return on equity,* and *liquidity ratio*. But you will need to define and explain those terms to a general audience.

Church leaders should be especially cautious with theological terms that are jargon to ordinary people. Telling the person on the street about *substitutionary atonement* won't mean as much as saying, "Christ died in your place." Talking about the *omnipresence, omniscience,* and *omnipotence* of God won't communicate as well as plainly saying that "God is everywhere, knows everything, and can do anything." The great truths of the faith deserve to be told as Jesus told them: in plain language for plain folks.

One final note on jargon: ordinary people harbor suspicions that a lot of jargon is concocted for the purpose of making what is simple appear complicated. Half of what I read and hear in the field of education these days falls into this category. (How else do you explain calling a school bus a *motorized attendance module* or the bus driver an *instructional facilitator*?) If your audience thinks you're trying to dazzle them with fifty-cent technical terms, they will remain both undazzled and unconvinced of anything you have to say.

Fillers.—Fillers are to speech what those little Styrofoam peanuts are to parcels: something to take up space. *All right, you know,* and the everpresent *OK?* are fillers. Even good words, such as *see, so,* or *now,* become fillers when they begin or end every other sentence. They are no longer a vital part of the thought you seek to express. They have become word wax.

Fillers are a form of word wax more often found in speaking than writing. Even if you never spot them when you write, beware. Using fillers is an easy habit to slip into. So, like try to, you know, avoid them when you speak, OK?

9. Address Your Listeners Directly

Prove by your words that your attention is focused on your listeners. Speak in the first and second person, not the third. Say *I, you, we, us, our, your.* Avoid *it, they, them, their.* By all means avoid the stuffy, pedantic style of address in which "*one* must watch *one's* words."

I heard of a church that called a bright young man fresh out of seminary to be their preacher. His sermons were works of great scholarship and erudition. But they were impersonal. His speech was directed to unspecified individuals or to third parties. *One* must do this or *one* must not do that. *The Christian, the believer, the child of God,* or somebody else was too often the subject of his sentences. He had marvelous things to say, but somehow he just never connected with the people in the room with him.

Determined that the young preacher needed to be more personal, the elders of the church met with him. One wise old fellow asked, "Preacher, do you know Homer Smith?"

"Yes I do," the preacher said, "he's the parishioner who works as an attendant at the corner service station."

"Well, Preacher," the elder continued, "what we need are sermons that will help Homer pump gas."

The young minister took their advice. In both his style and his content, he began to address his listeners directly. He even made up a plaque that he fastened to the back of the pulpit, placed so that he would see it each time he rose to preach. The plaque contained a single question: "Will it help Homer pump gas?"

Make both your content and your style of addressing your listeners personal. Strike a balance between being too formal and too familiar. Speak to your listeners much as you would in private conversation. Address them directly.

10. Keep It Simple

What did you have for breakfast this morning? "The upper portion of a domesticated hog's posterior appendage and two oval bodies encased in a shell laid by a female chicken" or "ham and eggs?" Keep it simple.

Whatever you have to say doesn't need to be complicated to be profound. At the height of his career, Jascha Heifetz was asked why no one had written a biography of him. The virtuoso violinist replied, "Here is my biography. I played the violin at three and gave my first concert at seven. I have been playing ever since." A simple style allows the real power of your ideas to splash undiluted onto your listeners' imaginations. Basic truths and events require simple language:

- Strike three.
- You're overdrawn.
- It's a boy!
- Yes.
- No.
- Walk.
- Don't walk.
- I love you.
- Jesus saves.

Several years ago, Robert Fulghum addressed a primary school celebration on the theme "All I Really Need to Know I Learned in Kindergarten." Senator Dan Evans heard the speech and later read a copy of it into the *Congressional Record*. It has since appeared in "Dear Abby" and the *Reader's Digest*, has been read over the radio by Paul Harvey and Larry King, and has found its way onto elementary school bulletin boards and refrigerator doors throughout the country. Much of the appeal of Fulghum's little piece is its profound simplicity. Listen:

> Most of what I really need to know about how to live and what to do and how to be I learned in kindergarten. Wisdom was not at the top of the graduate school mountain, but there in the sandpile at Sunday School. These are the things I learned:
> Share everything.
> Play fair.
> Don't hit people.
> Put things back where you found them.
> Clean up your own mess.
> Don't take things that aren't yours.
> Say you're sorry when you hurt somebody.
> Wash your hands before you eat.
> Flush.
> Warm cookies and cold milk are good for you.
> Live a balanced life—learn some and think some and draw and paint and sing and dance and play and work every day some.
> Take a nap every afternoon.
> When you go out into the world, watch for traffic, hold hands and stick together.
> Be aware of wonder[23]

Fulghum has since written a book bearing the title of

his popular speech. It is a delightful collection of essays on the everyday wonders of life. He writes about a shoe repairman who leaves cookies in the shoes he can't fix, a small deaf boy who wants to rake Fulghum's leaves, and the satisfaction of sorting laundry. It is not complicated stuff. He uses simple words. But his work enjoys an amazing popularity.

As long as what you have to say is significant, as long as it really is worth saying, then the simpler the terms you use to express your ideas, the better. Give your speaking style clarity and power. Keep it simple.

11. Be Clear

God didn't stop the building of the Tower of Babel with a thunderbolt. Instead He said, "Let us go down, and there confound their language, that they may not understand one another's speech" (Gen. 11:7, KJV). It stopped them cold. Fuzzy, inexact speech will stop your listeners, too.

Listeners have an economy of attention. They are not always so keen that they will dispel obscurities or ignore distractions without assistance. Just as sunlight forces itself upon the eyes, a speech should be so clear that our words thrust themselves into the listener's mind even when he is not following us closely. "Our aim," Quintilian says, "must be not to put him in a position to understand our argument, but to force him to understand it."

Too many speakers are infected with the notion that a speech which requires a commentator must, for that very reason, be a masterpiece of elegance. Don't believe it. Unless you say something your audience understands, you cannot possibly say something they will admire. Whatever else you do when you speak, you must be clear. A listener must be able to jump into your stream of words and emerge with the fish of a thought between his teeth.

Remember the three instructions Napoleon gave to his messengers. They were:

(1) Be clear!
(2) Be clear!
(3) Be clear!

Don't speak around your subject. Speak on it. Don't approximate. Be exact. Aim at speaking so clearly, so precisely, so unambiguously that your words can bear only one meaning. Be clear.

12. Make Good Use of the Wordsmith's Tools

Would you think much of a plumber who didn't own or know how to use a wrench? What about a carpenter who never came to work with a hammer? To do any job right you must have, know how to use, and use the right tools.

For a speaker or writer, the most important tool is a dictionary. There are no shortcuts. Anyone who hopes to use the English language accurately must make frequent use of a good college-level dictionary. It can tell you the meaning, spelling, pronunciation, and history of words you use, and, through usage notes and other helps, can guide you toward grace and precision in the use of your mother tongue. If used routinely, a good dictionary can insure that your speech will be that of an educated, well-informed adult. My preference is the college edition of the *American Heritage Dictionary*. The advice of the AHD's widely celebrated Usage Panel is incorporated in numerous usage notes throughout the dictionary. In these notes, outstanding writers, speakers, and thinkers offer their guidance in matters of style and usage.

As a public speaker you should keep your dictionary close at hand and use it daily. You need a dictionary at your elbow not only when you write, but when you read. I keep a dictionary on my office desk, another on my writing table in my study at home, and another on the nightstand by my bed, where I often read at night. You should acquire the habit of consulting a dictionary whenever you meet a word whose meaning, pronunciation, or usage is unfamiliar to you. There is no better method of mastering your language.

Mark Twain said the difference between the right word and almost the right word is like the difference between lightning and the lightning bug. Frequent use of a good thesaurus will help you find the right word to express your idea. *Webster's Collegiate Thesaurus* and *Webster's New Dictionary of Synonyms* are fine dictionary-style thesauri. The classic, and still the best, work in the field of synonyms is *Roget's International Thesaurus*, now in a fourth edition. I like *Roget's* because it groups words into related categories. You start by looking up a word in the index. The index will refer you to a numbered section in the book that contains synonyms for the word or idea you looked up. Along with synonyms for your word, you will also find related categories of words and phrases expressing similar ideas.

Another tool to keep on your writing table as you prepare your speeches is an English handbook. The *Harbrace College Handbook* and the *Holt Handbook* are both excellent guides to grammar and usage. If you're having trouble choosing the right form of a verb, making your subjects and predicates agree, or ordering your ideas in a good sentence, the help you need is in these books. Henry Fowler's *Modern English Usage* is a classic guide to good English. Wilson Follett's *Modern American Usage* and Eric Partridge's *Usage and Abusage: A Guide to Good English* are also excellent.

An almanac is another reference book that I keep several copies of in order to always have one wherever I'm writing. We discussed these handy general reference books of facts and figures in the first chapter on preparing speeches. To have both style and substance a speech needs plenty of specific, concrete information. That is why when I'm writing speeches I keep an almanac close by as a quick source of facts and details.

Summary

To effectively clothe your thought with words you must:
1. Speak to great issues.
2. Paint a picture for your listeners.
3. Be specific.
4. Use strong nouns and verbs
5. Use imaginative words.
6. Use the active voice.
7. Watch your grammar.
8. Avoid word wax.
9. Address your listeners directly.
10. Keep it simple.
11. Be clear.
12. Make good use of the wordsmith's tools.

Notes

1. Douglas MacArthur, "Duty, Honor, and Country," *Vital Speeches*, June 15, 1962, 519-21.

2. Peter Marshall, "Trumpet of the Morn," audio recording, *Peter Marshall Speaks*, Vol. 1 (New York: Caedmon, 1955).

3. Garrison Keillor, "Meeting Donny Hart at the Bus Stop," audio recording, *Gospel Birds and Other Stories of Lake Woebegon* (St. Paul: Minnesota Public Radio, 1985).

4. Garrison Keillor's books and tapes are currently sold across the country in book stores.

5. Peggy Noonan, *What I Saw at the Revolution* (New York: Random House, 1990), 79.

6. Billy Graham, Sermon on "Confusing Good with Evil," as cited in *The Wit and Wisdom of Billy Graham*, ed. Bill Adler (New York: Random House, 1967), 111.

7. E. B. White, *Elements of Style*, 2d ed. (New York: Macmillan, 1972), 64.

8. Garrison Keillor, *Lake Woebegon Days* (New York: Viking Penguin, 1985), 6.

9. Garrison Keillor, *Leaving Home* (New York: Viking Penguin, 1987), 17.

10. Keillor, *Lake Woebegon Days*, 135.

11. Ibid., 119.

12. Ibid., 83.

13. Keillor, *Leaving Home*, 74.

14. Garrison Keillor, *We Are Still Married* (New York: Viking Penguin, 1989), 71.

15. Pat Conroy, *Prince of Tides* (New York: Bantam Books, 1987), 464.

16. Ibid., 152.

17. Ibid., 146.

18. C. S. Lewis, *The Problem of Pain* (New York: Macmillan, 1962), 93, 95.

19. Richard Mitchell, *The Graves of Academe* (Boston: Little, Brown and Company, 1981) 65.

20. Norman Lewis, *Better English,* rev. ed. (New York: Dell Publishing Co., 1983).

21. The term "word wax" is from Richard C. Borden, *Public Speaking—As Listeners Like It!* (New York: Harper and Row, 1935).

22. James J. Kilpatrick, *The Writer's Art* (Kansas City: Andrews, McNeel and Parker, 1984), 5.

23. Robert Fulghum, *All I Really Need to Know I Learned in Kindergarten: Uncommon Thought on Common Things* (New York: Villard Books, 1988).

5

Speaking the Speech: Delivery

Speak the speech, I pray you, . . . trippingly on the tongue

—*Hamlet*

So they read from the book of the law of God distinctly, and gave the sense, and caused them to understand the reading (Neh. 8:8, KJV).

In *The Heart of Midlothian*, Sir Walter Scott tells the story of a young Scottish girl's efforts to save her sister from the gallows. Effie Deans had borne a child illegitimately and was convicted of murdering her baby to conceal his birth. Effie admitted the birth, but denied she had killed the child. She said she had fainted during labor and awoke to find that the midwife who attended her had disposed of the baby in some way unknown to Effie. Convicted of child murder, Effie was sentenced to be hanged.

Before the sentence could be carried out, Effie's sister, Jeanie, discovered who had taken the child and why. Determined to save her sister's life, Jeanie decided to walk from Edinburgh to London to seek a pardon from the king and queen. When she told her plans to her fiancé, he objected that the journey to London was too long and too dangerous. He pleaded with her to let him write a letter on Effie's behalf instead. But Jeanie would not be swayed: "We must try all means," replied Jeanie; "but writing winna do it—a letter canna look, and pray, and beg, and beseech, as the human voice can do to the human heart."[1]

The advantage of speech over the written word is what the human voice can do to the human heart. Two millennia before Sir Walter put those words in the mouth of his young Scottish character, Plato observed that "it is the speech of the man who knows that is alive: the written word is really but its ghost."

So far, most of the rules for speakers we have discussed apply equally to the work of writers. The makers of books and makers of speeches must both observe common rules of substance, organization, and style. In this chapter we will observe some important distinctions in delivering your ideas through the human voice.

1. Know Your Speech

Before the Battle of El Alamein, Winston Churchill summoned General Montgomery to discuss some logistical details of the battle. Montgomery doubted that he should become involved in such detailed technical matters. "After all," he said, "you know what they say, familiarity breeds contempt."

Churchill replied, "I would like to remind you that without a degree of familiarity, we could not breed anything."

Knowing your speech is not the most important rule of delivery, but it comes first because you cannot observe the others if you break this one. You must be thoroughly familiar with the structure and content of your speech in order to concentrate on delivering it well. Try driving from Baltimore to Atlanta, or even a hundred yards in any direction, with your nose stuck in a map the whole time. A driver must know his route well enough to keep his eyes on the road, referring to the map from time to time to refresh his memory.

Most good speakers use notes when they speak. But

they memorize the structure and enough of the supporting material in the speech to keep the notes from becoming the focus of their attention. The notes are a map, not a script.

For many beginning speakers there is a more crucial reason for knowing the speech before you speak. Lack of adequate preparation is the greatest single cause of stage fright. And, frankly, if you are unprepared, you deserve to be scared. But, if you've done your homework, if you have thoroughly researched and analyzed your topic, if you are prepared to enter into an intelligent discussion of your subject, then you should stand up and speak with confidence. You have earned the right to give that speech!

Work on memorizing the ideas, not the words of your speech. Carry in your head the outline of what you wish to say and let the words come to your tongue as you look into the faces of your listeners.

2. Speak with Passion

James Madison was one of the most active speakers at the Constitutional Convention of 1787. Concerned that he tended to get carried away when he addressed the convention, Madison asked a friend seated near him to pull on his coattails if he seemed to become overexcited as he spoke. Following a particularly impassioned speech, an exhausted Madison sat down and admonished his friend for not pulling at his coat. His friend replied, "I would as soon have laid my finger on the lightning."

Madison had what modern political observers call "fire in the belly." It is an essential quality for leadership in any arena, especially on the speaking platform.

By the time you reach the delivery stage, your commitment to and passion for the cause you represent are assumed. Let that passion flow from your heart and mind out through the ends of your tongue and fingers.

To be a great speaker requires more than saying something well. It means doing something. It means becoming the living arena in which the idea or cause for which you speak confronts your listeners. Remember that the one essential of a great delivery is a genuine conviction about and feeling for your cause. Without it, no other skill in speaking is of value. With it, a multitude of faults will be overlooked.

The nineteenth-century rhetorician Richard Whately illustrated the principle with this story: A preacher once asked a popular actor why people listened to him with so much interest and emotion while he spoke fictitious lines that, even if true, were of no personal concern to them; yet they listened to the preacher with comparative apathy while he spoke the most sublime truths that were of eternal significance to them. The actor answered, "Because we deliver fiction like it was truth, and you deliver truth like it was fiction."

3. See What You Say

The ancient Greeks taught that the pinnacle of great speaking is the absorption of the audience into the speech. It is not enough that you possess a passion for the ideas in your speech. Your listeners must be caught up with you. They, too, must lose themselves in what you are saying.

The Greeks called this absorption of the audience into the speech *ekstasis*. The word describes a state of emotion so intense that the listener is carried beyond himself (*ek* "out of" + *stasis* "place"). It is the root of our

English word *ecstasy*. A good speech should convince and please the audience. But a great speech does that and more. It transports the listeners beyond themselves and absorbs them into something bigger than they are.

The key to absorbing the audience into the speech is painting vivid mental images in their minds. But you cannot paint a picture for them that you have not seen yourself. You cannot push an audience into a speech. You must first get in, then pull them in after you. You must have an intense, concrete realization of what you say as you say it. Translate your convictions and commitment to the subject into vivid mental images, then describe those images to your listeners. The aim is for the audience not only to hear, but to sense what you say.

Avoid thinking of yourself when speaking and confine the powers of your mind to the object of the speech itself. Concentrate on the meaning behind each word you speak. Try to see, hear, feel, taste, and smell what you are describing to your listeners. Once these inner images have stirred the appropriate feelings and mood within you, only then are you ready to arouse those same feelings within your audience.

Great speeches come from speakers who lose themselves in their topics, who vividly sense what they say, and who aim not at a mere narration of facts, but at a living display of truth before the eyes of their listeners' minds.

4. Keep Your Eyes on Your Audience

Concerned that he might commit some slip of the tongue, a nervous young preacher delivered the first sermon at his new church by reading a manuscript. After services, an elderly lady remarked to her friend that she didn't like the sermon at all. "Why not?" asked the lady's companion.

"Well, first of all," she answered, "he read the sermon. Second, he didn't read it very well. And, finally, it wasn't worth reading."

Effective speakers look their listeners in the eye for two reasons. First, your audience expects you to look at them. People lose confidence in a speaker who cannot or will not look them in the eye. You must establish a visual bond with your listeners. Second, even formal platform speaking is a two-way process. Looking at your listeners tells you when you're doing well and when you're not. It enables you to adapt to your audience as you speak. It also heightens your energy and excitement by constantly reminding you that this is not a test, but a live appearance before a room full of real people.

Good eye contact has two parts: looking at all your listeners and actually seeing them. Don't play favorites with your eye contact. Look at all your listeners. Make the man by the back door feel as much a part of what you're doing on the platform as the lady in the center seat on the front row. And take care to see your listeners as individuals rather than a composite blur. Focus upon a given listener so that he will say to himself, "The next time this speaker sees me he'll recognize me." Follow the example of the apostle Paul who "looked straight at the Sanhedrin" when he appeared before them (Acts 23:1.)

5. Speak Clearly

Have you ever read a book or newspaper with missing or misprinted letters? If you made it past the irritation of having to guess what the writer said, and if you had the time and tried hard enough, you may have been able to reach some understanding of the meaning behind the misprinted words.

If you mumble or slur your words when you speak, the listener has no recourse as he might have with a badly printed book. He cannot bring the words back to try to figure out what you said. The speech plunges forward, leaving your listener in the dark. You must speak clearly. Being understood on the platform begins with the effective use of those parts of your body used in producing speech.

Start your voice at your belt, not your throat.—The power for driving your voice must come not from your throat, but from below it. Victorian actors called this "packing your tones against your belt." Standing erect, inhale by expanding your abdomen rather than your chest. The idea is to draw a deep breath into the lungs by pulling down on the diaphragm. As you speak, use the muscles of your abdomen to push the air out in a steady stream. Be sure to maintain enough breath that you avoid running out of air before your next breath. The main thing to remember is that an effective voice is produced by a push from the gut, not the throat.

Relax your throat.—The actual sound produced by your vocal cords is too feeble to be heard at any distance. It is weak and lacks carrying power. The voice does not become strong and rich until it is amplified by the resonators in your throat and head. As the air in a drum amplifies its sound, so your pharynx, trachea, mouth, nose, and sinuses amplify and enrich your voice. To speak well from the platform, these resonators must be relaxed. Forcing sounds out through a constricted throat will produce a strained, unpleasant voice. It will

also soon result in hoarseness or more serious problems. Let your abdomen do the pushing and allow the
sounds to glide and resonate up through your throat.

Articulate your syllables clearly.—Your articulators
(the palate, tongue, teeth, and lips) are responsible for
the final shape of your words. Careless, sluggish articulation results in slurred, garbled speech. Listen to yourself carefully. Do you say things like:

- *Dunno* for *don't know*,
- *Whassat* for *what's that*,
- *Nutin* for *nothing*,
- *Gimme* for *give me*,
- *Gunna* for *going to*?

If you fail to articulate all the sounds that make up
your words, your listeners may not understand everything you say. Even when they do make out what you
said, your speech will sound lazy and inelegant.

Good articulation depends on three things. First, you
must make up your mind to use your tongue and lips to
shape your words correctly. Most people have no trouble speaking clearly once they have actually decided to
make their mouths take an active part in forming their
words. Keep your tongue and lips alive and flexible
while you speak.

Second, open your mouth wide enough to let the
words out. Pushing your words out through a half-shut
slit will garble your speech. I have known many mum-
blers who were perfectly capable of speaking clearly
once they opened their mouths wider when speaking.
Pay special attention to opening wide for vowel sounds:
A, E, I, O, U, and the various combinations of these
sounds. They supply most of the volume in speaking.
To be heard you must open up and let the vowels out.

Third, pay careful attention to the individual sounds in words. Vowels are the river of speech, consonants the banks. If you cut short the full sound due the vowels, the river dries up. If you fail to articulate the consonants, the river overflows its banks and your words are sucked into the marsh and lost. Pay attention to the individual vowels and consonants of your words.

Put enough breath behind your consonants to make them clearly heard no matter where they come in a word. Put pressure on initial consonants, such as the *p* in *profit*, the *t* in *talk*, or the *k* in *kick*. Pay attention to consonants in the middle of words: say *twenty*, not *twenny*, *started*, not *starded*. Sound out the ends of your words: put the *t* on *don't*, the *s* on *yes*, and the *l* on *pull*. Hold long consonants long enough to get them going. It takes a moment to build up the *r* in *rough*, the *n* in *now*, or the *l* in *will*.

Beware of slipping over little words, such as articles and prepositions. Speak them distinctly. Don't let your voice trail off toward the end of a word or the end of a sentence. Keep the volume up all the way to the end.

Whether vowel or consonant, take care to enunciate each sound of each syllable of each word distinctly. Don't slur your words. Give every syllable its due. Don't hurry over, drop, or crowd together syllables. Avoid running your words together, so as to make two or more words sound like one. If you want to learn more about improving your speaking voice, Lyle V. Mayer's *Fundamentals of Voice and Diction* is an excellent guide.[2]

One final hint: your listeners will find it helpful if you speak from the front of your mouth. Singers and actors call this placing the voice "in the mask." A sound that is laid against the teeth and bones in the front of the mouth acquires a ring and power that is lacking in sounds that are allowed to fall against the soft palate or the back of the throat. Form your words as far forward in the mouth as you comfortably can without distorting them.

Pronounce your words correctly.—Whether you like it or not, your audience will judge you and the worth of your ideas by whether you can correctly pronounce the words you use. Never use a word you don't *know* how to pronounce. If you are unsure, look it up. The speaker who is foolish enough to guess at the pronunciation of a word that he is too lazy to look it up is just asking to be embarrassed.

There are four ways to mispronounce a word: by omitting, adding, or transposing letters or syllables, or by stressing the wrong syllable. Omission of letters turns *everybody* into *everbody*, *library* into *libary*, and *recognize* into *reconize*. The careless addition of letters turns *athlete* into *ath-uh-lete*, *hindrance* into *hin-der-ance*, and *disastrous* into *dis-as-ter-ous*. The transposition of letters turns *children* into *child-der-en*, *cavalry* into *cal-va-ry*, and *prefer* into *per-fer*. Misplacing the stress in a word can make *ce*-ment of *cement* or *po*-lice of *police*.

A good college-level dictionary, such as the *American Heritage Dictionary*, is an indispensable tool for knowing the correct way to say the words in your speech. Most dictionaries have a key to the pronunciation symbols at the bottom of each page as well as in the introductory pages at the front of the dictionary. Acquire the habit of consulting a dictionary whenever you must use a word whose meaning, usage, or pronunciation is unfamiliar to you.

6. Speak Animatedly

In 1954 the National Basketball Association was in trouble. Attendance at games was low, fans were bored, and many franchises were losing money. The problem? The game had become dull. Basketball fans like to see plenty of shooting and scoring. But the rules did nothing to encourage teams with a lead to shoot the ball. A team that was leading late in the game would pass the ball to their best ball handler, who would dribble away the clock in the backcourt. There was no incentive for a team with the lead to run the ball down court, set up their offense, and shoot.

All that changed in the 1954-55 season when the NBA introduced the twenty-four-second shot clock. The clock compelled each team to shoot the ball within twenty-four seconds of coming into possession of it. The new rule revolutionized the game. At least once every twenty-four seconds of play something was going to change. Somebody was going to score, rebound, or turn over the ball. The fans loved it.

Audiences are like basketball spectators. They can't stand monotony. When you speak, your listeners want to hear an animated voice that sparkles with variety and expression. The key to keeping your voice from becoming dull and monotonous is change, change in pitch, volume, and rate.

Change of pitch.—Unless your voice has some variety in its pitch, you will lull your subjects into a hypnotic trance. Remember, you're a speaker, not a hypnotist. Your goal is to awaken your audience, not drone them to sleep. The thoughtful intonation of words can color them with varied shades of feeling. Let your voice rise in a natural inflection to suggest doubt, suspense, uncertainty, or interrogation. Let it fall to suggest firmness, certainty, or finality.

You also have control over the rate at which you change your pitch and the size of the steps between the various pitches. Restrained moods such as reverence, grief, or nobility are best expressed by narrow changes in pitch. Spirited moods such as anger, surprise, or delight are best expressed by wider steps in pitch.

Change of volume.—Your overall volume should be sufficient to make yourself heard. Speak too softly and people will not hear you or, if they do, they will think you are unsure of or uncommitted to what you are saying. Once your volume reaches a sufficient level to communicate your ideas with force and vigor, increasing or decreasing the loudness of a word or phrase can make it stand out. Notice the subtle changes in meaning that come from stressing different words in a sentence:

- *What* did you say to her? (A straight question.)
- What *did* you say to her? (You provoked her in some fashion.)
- What did *you* say to her? (You personally, not someone else.)
- What did you *say* to her? (What you *did* is another matter.)
- What did you say *to her*? (Not to me or to him, but to her.)

Vocal emphasis adds meaning to your speech. Variety in volume can keep an attentive audience or reawaken a drowsy one.

Change of rate.—If you've ever ridden a sight-seeing bus you may have noticed that as it passes a row of plain houses, it speeds up. When it comes to an important building, it slows down. Occasionally, before a historic landmark, it comes to a complete stop. Imitate the technique of the sightseeing bus in your rate of delivery.

Some sentences should be spoken slowly and emphatically, giving the listeners time to gather the sense of what you are saying. Others demand a livelier pace. Use variety in your rate of speaking, but observe the minimum and maximum speed limits (roughly 100 to 200 words per minute). Speak slowly enough that you are intelligible, but not so slowly that people begin to shake their watches.

Your voice is a flexible instrument capable of expressing fine shades of meaning and emotion. Use your full range of pitch, volume, and rate to hold your listeners' interest with an animated voice.

7. Put Your Pauses to Good Use

A group of Arabs from the Sahara desert were visiting Niagara Falls. Unaccustomed to seeing such a huge volume of water pour over the edge of a cliff, they stood watching the falls for what seemed to the tour guide an interminable time. Finally, the guide asked what they were waiting for. One of the Arabs relied, "We're waiting to see it stop."

Audiences, too, will be waiting to hear you stop when you speak. Pauses are to speaking what punctuation is to writing. Acquire a thorough familiarity with the use of stops in speaking.

• Howlongwouldyoucontinuetoreadabookthatranall thewordstogetherwithnospacesorpunctuationbetween them?

In speaking, as in writing, the spaces between your

words are as important as the words themselves. Actually, the use of spaces or pauses between words and phrases is more important to speaking than to writing.

Poorly placed pauses can hack a good speech to death. Use the spaces between your words as punctuation marks, not hatchets. Let your pauses fall between thoughts or phrases, not in the middle of them. A pause before a key idea or the climax of a story can add suspense. A pause immediately after an important point adds emphasis. Properly timed, a dramatic break or delay in the flow of words can do more to express your meaning than the words themselves.

Avoid vocalized pauses. When you stop, do it clearly: no er-r-rs, um-m-ms, uh-h-hs, or OKs. These annoying vocal fillers distract the listener from what you are saying. Don't be afraid to pause, and don't think you need to fill the gaps with meaningless syllables.

8. Talk from Your Toes Up

Henry Ward Beecher advised: "When people fall asleep in church, awaken the man in the pulpit." No one is interested in listening to a statue that moves its lips. You must be completely involved in your speech. Don't bore your listeners with a talking head. Show them there is something going on up on the platform. Show them they are listening to a person of action with an idea so compelling he has to use his whole self to tell them about it. Show them that you know their time is valuable, that you appreciate this opportunity to address them, and that you intend to stay on your toes and alertly use all your physical resources for as long as you claim their time. Maintain an alert, balanced body carriage throughout the speech.

Good gestures can add great force to your speaking.

During the turbulent century between the old Roman republic and the empire, Cicero rose to prominence as the greatest orator of ancient Rome. So formidable were the powers of his eloquence, that Octavian, who would later become Caesar Augustus, realized that the Roman constitution could not be abolished until he had silenced Cicero permanently. Following Cicero's execution, his enemies displayed his tongue and hands on the speakers' rostrum at the Roman Forum. In a cruel fashion they acknowledged the power of Cicero's voice *and gestures* as an orator. Fortunately, his fate is not common among public speakers these days. Still, the power of well-executed gestures in speaking remains.

It is odd that many people who think nothing of talking with their hands in normal conversation have no idea what to do with them when they give a speech. Let your hands describe and punctuate what you say with appropriate gestures, much as you would when talking with friends. Follow the example of the apostle Paul who "stretched out his hands" as he spoke to the crowd at the temple (Acts 21:40, author). But don't overdo it. Gesture with discrimination. Shakespeare tucked away some excellent advice on gestures in *Hamlet*: "Do not saw the air too much with your hand, thus; but use all gently. . . . Be not too tame neither, but let your own discretion be your tutor: suit the action to the word, the word to the action."[3]

Every motion on the platform must serve a purpose. Along with your tone of voice, your facial expressions and gestures account for 90 percent of the meaning your listeners receive when you speak. Take care to suit each gesture to the word it is to describe or punctuate.

9. Speak with Poise

I was on the floor of the 1984 Republican National Convention when actor Charlton Heston came forward to lead the pledge of allegiance. There was no introduction. The chairman simply said, "Ladies and gentlemen, Mr. Charlton Heston of California will now lead us in the Pledge of Allegiance to the flag." At this announcement, the crowd erupted in applause and cheers. When the renowned actor reached the podium, he neither did nor said anything to acknowledge the ovation. He simply paused, looked straight at the audience, and placed his hand over his heart. The effect of his manner and bearing upon the crowd was immediate. As the first words fell from his lips, several thousand people stood in reverent silence, then joined him in the pledge. The reason? Heston had presence. He possessed a dignity and grace that demanded respectful attention.

Granted, it doesn't hurt his deportment to have played Moses in *The Ten Commandments*, but don't use that as an excuse not to develop your own poise and presence on the platform. There is no complicated ritual to developing an alert, balanced body carriage. Keep your center of gravity balanced on both feet. Don't shift your weight from foot to foot. Your head and body should be erect, but not stiff. Don't slouch. Do nothing that makes you look lazy or not fully alert. Aim at looking relaxed, but not casual; animated, but not agitated.

By all means, be enthusiastic. Use your face, hands, and body to express yourself energetically. But bridle your drive and vitality with a touch of dignity and restraint. Speak with poise.

One last suggestion on poise. Act like you belong on

the platform. No matter how nervous or out of place you may feel inside, take charge of your audience. Whenever I feel unsettled by a strange audience or situation I remember how John Tyler, the first Vice-President to succeed a President who died in office, handled himself. In 1841 the constitution lacked a clear provision to guide presidential succession, and there was considerable disagreement in Washington as to whether Tyler should succeed William Henry Harrison or merely hold the office until the congress decided how to choose a new, permanent President.

Tyler decided that he did indeed have the right to assume the office and proceeded to exercise the powers and perform the duties of the President. Political opponents in the congress and the administration sent important messages to the White House addressed to "Hon. John Tyler, Acting President." President Tyler refused even to open any letters addressed in that fashion. Because he acted like the President, people came to regard him as such. He set a powerful precedent that was followed thereafter, though it did not formally become part of the Constitution until ratification of the Twenty-fifth Amendment in 1967.

Usually when you speak, you are on the platform because the people to whom you are speaking expect you to be up there. Act like you belong behind the podium. Act like your knowledge of and commitment to the subject at hand have earned you the right to be there. Keep a proper sense of humility and don't take your audience for granted, but at the same time assume the rightful authority that is yours as a capable, informed speaker.

10. Make Your Motions Meaningful

If you're nervous when you rise to speak—good! It means that your batteries are charged. Nervous energy is part of the difference between a racehorse and a cow.

Cows are not nervous creatures. They don't fret, they don't rush, and they don't appear to care whether anyone watches them graze, sleep, or moo. Racehorses, however, are high-strung. They are wild-eyed creatures who enter their starting gates literally chomping at the bit. They are not to be kept waiting. As soon as the last horse is in place, the starting bell sounds and they burst from their gates. They are full of a nervous impatience to race. Their nervous energy is purposefully expended in something we call the sport of kings.

Chihuahuas, too, are nervous creatures. But theirs is the haggard, neurotic shivering of a nervous little animal that one would comfort or pamper, but not admire.

You don't want to be a cow or a Chihuahua, but a racehorse. You don't need to get rid of the butterflies in your stomach, just make them fly in formation. Channel your nervousness away from distracting mannerisms into an energetic delivery.

Specifically: Don't shuffle your feet. Don't rattle the change in your pocket. Don't fidget. Don't groom yourself. Don't play with the podium, your notes, or anything else within reach. Don't lean on the podium. Do nothing that calls attention to itself.

11. Look the Part

Shakespeare said, "Clothes doth oft proclaim the man." Most of the authority figures in our lives are identified by some kind of distinctive plumage. If the man in a sharply pressed uniform wearing a pistol and a badge directs you to stop your car in the middle of the street, you probably will and follow whatever other instructions the policeman gives you.

Though we do not usually think of a suit and tie as a uniform, it is. A traditional, conservative suit is a positive symbol of authority. Such suits are worn by the people who make most of the important decisions in our lives. Like it or not, people are more likely to believe, respect, and obey the person who dresses the part. This is especially true for public speaking. John T. Molloy has written two excellent books on how clothing affects the wearer's influence upon other people: *Dress for Success* and *The Woman's Dress for Success Book*.[4] Both are worth a place in the successful speaker's library.

As a public speaker your overall look should be traditional, conservative, and neat. The platform is not the place to make a high-fashion statement or to show off your sex appeal. The perfect speaker's outfit for a gentleman is a navy or gray wool or wool-blend suit, a white or light blue Oxford button-down shirt, and a conservative-patterned silk or silk-blend tie. Splurge on the tie. It's the most important status symbol in your outfit. The end of the tie should be long enough to touch your belt buckle, but no longer. Unless you are in formal dress, never wear a bow tie.

Make sure everything fits. The waist of your pants should be slightly above your navel. Your pants cuffs should be as long as possible without dragging the floor. Nothing—pants, jacket, or shirt—should be tight enough to pull or loose enough to bulge. Actually, a properly fitted shirt and suit not only look better, but will make you more comfortable when you speak.

Wear traditional lace shoes, black or cordovan, preferably wing tips and definitely shined. Get a neat haircut and, except for a wedding band or a class ring, lose the jewelry.

For ladies a dark, skirted suit with a white or pastel blouse works best. A contrasting scarf is acceptable. Natural colored hose and simple pumps finish out your speaking uniform. Aim at looking feminine but businesslike. Again, save your sex appeal for off-platform appearances.

If you're on a limited budget, don't excuse yourself from putting together the right look because you think it's too expensive. It's not. Well-fitted, conservative-colored, upper-class looking suits come in a wide range of prices. Time invested in shopping for and fitting a good suit will pay off on the platform.

12. Be Brief

On March 4, 1841, President William Henry Harrison stood without a hat or coat in a cold drizzle and delivered the longest inaugural speech on record: one hour and forty-five minutes. Harrison caught a cold, came down with pneumonia, and on April 4, died after serving only one month in office.

There are two lessons in that story. One is to wear a hat and coat in bad weather. The other lesson is to *make your speeches brief.* If President Harrison had dressed for the season, he might have survived. But at 8,578 words, the speech would probably have still died. (I've read the speech. Better that *it* should have died of pneumonia.)

Remember, your audience wants you to do two things: first, they want you to speak well. Then, they want you to sit down. During the speech it is your job to talk and theirs to listen. It's a good idea to finish your job before they finish theirs. Make the total speech and every part of the speech as brief as possible. I've yet to hear a listener complain because the speaker didn't keep him long enough. The ideal time for a speech is twenty minutes. Don't keep them longer than thirty minutes at the outside. As my Aunt Sarah, one of the world's greatest living speech critics, says of long sermons: "If you can't strike oil in twenty minutes, quit drilling!" Good speakers know when to quit.

Follow the example of Jonathan Swift. While dean of Saint Patrick's in Dublin, he received complaints over an inordinately long sermon on stewardship. He determined to make his next sermon on that topic concise. He announced his text as Proverbs 19:17, "He that hath pity upon the poor lendeth unto the Lord; and that which he hath given will he pay him again."

"You have heard the terms of the loan," Swift said, "and if you like the terms, put down your money."

He then sat down. The resulting donations were generous. A speech doesn't have to be long to be effective. Be brief.

Summary

The most eloquent statesman of ancient Athens, Demosthenes, was once asked to name the three most important aspects of persuasive speaking. "The first," he answered, "is delivery. And the second is delivery."

"And the third?" his questioner inquired.

"Delivery," came the reply.

Demosthenes knew that great thoughts move us far more when heard than when read and that ideas often secure a hearing on the platform that is denied them in the library. If you would convince others of the rightness of your cause, master the rules of delivery:

1. Know your speech.
2. Speak with passion.
3. See what you say.
4. Keep your eyes on your audience.
5. Speak clearly.
6. Speak animatedly.
7. Put your pauses to good use.
8. Talk from your toes up.
9. Speak with poise.
10. Make your motions meaningful.
11. Look the part.
12. Be brief.

When a great idea is coupled with a powerful delivery, it scatters everything before it like a bolt of lightning. Let experience and attention to the rules of good speaking sharpen your abilities. Dedicate yourself to learning to ignite your ideas with the fire that voice, look, and action can give them.

Notes

1. Sir Walter Scott, *The Heart of Midlothian* (London: J. M. Dent and Sons, 1906), 290.

2. Lyle V. Mayer, *Fundamentals of Voice and Diction,* 7th ed. (Dubuque, Iowa: William C. Brown, 1985).

3. Act III, scene 2.

4. A paperback edition is now available under the title *John T. Molloy's New Dress for Success* (New York: Warner Books, 1988).